SCHOLASTIC

NO FUSS

ENGLISH
PHOTOCOPIABLES
AGES 5-7

LEVELS

1-3

- Levelled and linked to the curriculum

- Stand-alone photocopiable activities

- Ideal for mixed classes

Compiled by Alison Milford

NO FUSS

UNIVERSITY OF CHICHESTER

CONTRIBUTORS

Text © **Diana Bentley and Dee Reid**: 26, 27, 31, 64, 76, 81, 83, 85, 87, 91, 92, 112, 115

Text © **Diana Bentley and Jane Whitwell**: 84, 86

Text © **Philip Bowditch**: 90, 94, 95, 97, 98, 99, 100, 101, 102

Text © **Kate Caton**: 16, 66, 93, 107, 111, 125, 127

Text © **William Edmonds**: 38, 39, 48, 49, 65, 96, 119, 120

Text © **Norma Gaunt and Jane Whitwell**: 53, 106, 108, 109, 110, 114, 118, 121, 122, 123, 124, 126

Text © **Wendy Helsby**: 15, 43, 44, 45, 103

Text © **Stephanie Mudd & Hilary Mason**: 17, 18, 19, 20, 21, 22, 23, 25, 28, 29, 30, 32, 33, 34, 36, 37, 40, 41

Text © **Rita Ray**: 24, 47, 67, 68, 69, 70, 71, 72, 73, 74, 75, 77, 78, 79, 80, 82, 88, 89, 105, 113, 116, 117

Text © **Angela Redfern**: 35, 42, 46, 50, 51, 52, 54, 55, 56, 57, 58, 59, 60, 61, 62, 63, 104

CONSULTANT EDITOR
Alison Milford

ASSISTANT EDITOR
Wendy Tse

DESIGNERS
Lapiz Digital

COVER DESIGN
Anna Oliwa

ILLUSTRATORS

Illustration © **Gaynor Berry**: 26, 27, 31, 64, 76, 81, 83, 84, 85, 86, 87, 91, 92

Illustration © **Sue Cony**: 53, 108, 110, 118, 121, 122, 124

Illustration © **Garry Davies**: 24, 47, 67, 68, 69, 70, 71, 72, 73, 74, 75, 77, 78, 79, 80, 82, 88, 89, 105, 113, 116, 117

Illustration © **Roger Fereday**: 90, 94, 95, 97, 98, 99, 100, 101, 102

Illustration © **Lorna Kent**: 17, 18, 19, 20, 21, 22, 23, 25, 28, 29, 30, 32, 33, 34, 36, 37, 40, 41

Illustration © **Oxford Illustrators**: 15, 43, 44, 45, 50, 51, 52, 54, 55, 56, 57, 58, 59, 60, 61, 62, 63, 103

Illustration © **Lesley Smith**: 16, 66, 93, 107, 111, 125, 127

Illustration © **Liz Thomas**: 35, 38, 39, 42, 46, 48, 49, 65, 96, 104, 119, 120

Illustration © **Jenny Tulip**: 106, 109, 112, 114, 115, 123, 126

Text and illustration copyright in individual pages as per acknowledgements.
Compilation © 2006 Scholastic Ltd

Every effort has been made to trace all the copyright owners of material but there were a few cases where an author or illustrator was untraceable. Scholastic will be happy to correct any omissions in future printings.

Published by Scholastic Ltd
Villiers House
Clarendon Avenue
Leamington Spa
Warwickshire
CV32 5PR

www.scholastic.co.uk

Designed using Adobe InDesign

Printed by Bell & Bain Ltd, Glasgow

6789   9012345

British Library Cataloguing-in-Publication Data

A catalogue record for this book is available from the British Library.

ISBN 0-439-96548-9

ISBN 978-0439-96548-4

Extracts from the National Literacy Strategy reproduced under the terms of HMSO Guidance Note 8. © Crown copyright.

Photocopiable pages and original teachers' notes first published in *Dictionary skills, Reading for comprehension, Reading non-fiction* and *Writing non-fiction* (all first published 1994) from the Essentials for English series, and *Grammar* (1997), *Handwriting activities* (1993), *Language puzzles* (1993), *Spelling and language skills* (1993), *Story writing* (1997), *Vocabulary skills* (1995) and *Writing* (1992) from the Teacher Timesavers series.

CR 428 NO

NO FUSS

SCHOLASTIC
www.scholastic.co.uk

FSC

Mixed Sources
Product group from well-managed forests and other controlled sources
www.fsc.org Cert no. TT-COC-002769
© 1996 Forest Stewardship Council

NO FUSS

CONTENTS

CONTENTS

CHAPTER 3
COMPREHENSION AND COMPOSITION – FICTION AND POETRY

CHAPTER 4
COMPREHENSION AND COMPOSITION – NON-FICTION

SCHOLASTIC
www.scholastic.co.uk

INTRODUCTION

This book contains over 100 of some of the best literacy photocopiable sheets compiled from past editions of Scholastic's popular series Essentials for English and Teacher Timesavers. The photocopiable sheets cover a wide range of literacy skills for five- to seven-year-olds and can be used by individuals, small groups or as class activities.

Aims of the book

• To offer fun and stimulating activities that encourage children to learn a range of literacy skills.

• To provide accessible activities that cover the literacy requirements for children aged five to seven.

• To provide activities that can be used for children of different abilities.

• To stimulate children into learning and discovering more about a skill or concept.

• To provide simple and interesting activities that can be used as an introduction to a lesson or skill or as a way of consolidating skills and knowledge.

• To be used as a resource that can be incorporated quickly and effectively into a busy timetable.

• To offer activities that could be used as forms of assessment.

• To act as a resource that offers good-quality activities to fill in an unplanned time slot.

Using the book

The activities: The photocopiable activities in this book are arranged in the order of the three levels of the National Literacy Strategy – Word level work, Sentence level work and Text level work. The chapters cover: Phonics, spelling and vocabulary; Grammar and punctuation; Comprehension and composition – fiction and poetry; Comprehension and composition – non-fiction. The activities progress throughout the chapters to match the children's development.

Curriculum grids: At the beginning of the book there are sets of curriculum grids which provide quick and easy-to-read information about each of the photocopiable activities. Each curriculum grid has seven sections:

Page number: This column indicates the page number of an activity for quick reference.

Activity: This column highlights the title of the activity.

Objective: This column highlights the specific objectives of an activity and what the children should be aiming to achieve.

Teachers' notes: This column gives teachers advice about how to use an activity with the children. This could include how children should be using the activity, ways to introduce the activity, ways to extend the activity once it has been completed or ideas for differentiation.

Curriculum links: The last three columns give direct links to the relevant Government documents for the NLS and Scottish curriculum and attainment target levels for each activity. These links can help teachers include the activities in their planning, assessment and with the development of ideas for future relevant activities.

It has been fun compiling some of Scholastic's best photocopiable English activities and we hope you and the children have just as much fun and enjoyment using them.

Page	Activity	Objective	Teachers' notes	National Literacy Strategy links	Scottish Curriculum links	KS1 Levels
page 15	A letter bird	To recognise the capital and small letters of the alphabet.	This puzzle helps to reinforce alphabetical order. The letter bird is made up of the letters V, M, E, U, O, J, Y, W.	Y1 T1 Word 2	Writing: Spelling – Level A	AT2 Reading – Level 1 AT3 Writing – Level 1
page 16	Alphabet Arthur	To reinforce a good knowledge of the alphabet.	A good activity to use in work on the alphabet. It requires some concentration, as the letters are not going from left to right.	Y1 T1 Word 2	Writing: Spelling – Level A	AT2 Reading – Level 1 AT3 Writing – Level 1
page 17	Pink butterfly	To put the correct initial letter sounds at the beginning of words and recognise the words they have made.	The whole butterfly should be coloured. Let children find classroom objects that also begin with the sounds 'b' and 'p'.	Y1 T2 Word 1	Writing: Spelling – Level A	AT2 Reading – Level 1 AT3 Writing – Level 1
page 18	Carl the cat	To recognise objects beginning with the letter sounds 'c' and 'g'.	Highlight shapes containing pictures of things beginning with 'g'. Ask children why the model is called Carl the cat.	Y1 T2 Word 1	Writing: Spelling – Level A	AT2 Reading – Level 1 AT3 Writing – Level 1
page 19	Can you find Tom?	To recognise objects beginning with the letter sounds 'd' and 't'.	To help children hear the difference between the two sounds, play odd one out by calling out objects with 't' letter sounds and adding in one 'd' sound.	Y1 T2 Word 1	Writing: Spelling – Level A	AT2 Reading – Level 1 AT3 Writing – Level 1
page 20	Moving day	To put the correct initial letter sounds at the beginning of words and recognise the words they have made.	Share 'moving day' experiences. Ask children to think of objects with 'f' or 'v' sounds that could be packed in a removal van.	Y1 T2 Word 1	Writing: Spelling – Level A	AT2 Reading – Level 1 AT3 Writing – Level 1
page 21	Sort the toys	To write and recognise objects beginning with the letters 'h', 'j' and 'm'.	Before children start this activity, go through the starting letter sounds of the toys.	Y1 T2 Word 1	Writing: Spelling – Level A	AT2 Reading – Level 1 AT3 Writing – Level 1
page 22	Robot's walk	To recognise objects beginning with the letter sounds 'r' and 'w'.	To help children work out the right track, ask them to colour in the objects beginning with the letter 'r' in red first.	Y1 T2 Word 1	Writing: Spelling – Level A	AT2 Reading – Level 1 AT3 Writing – Level 1
page 23	What's my name?	To put the correct initial letter sounds at the beginning of words and recognise the words they have made.	Explain the idea behind acrostics. Highlight how the first letter of the boy's name is a capital letter.	Y1 T2 Word 1	Writing: Spelling – Level A	AT2 Reading – Level 1 AT3 Writing – Level 1
page 24	Find the vowels	To recognise the five vowels.	Highlight that each word in the flag has one or more vowels.	Y1 T2 Word 1	Writing: Spelling – Level A	AT2 Reading – Level 1 AT3 Writing – Level 1
page 25	Hide and seek	To discriminate and hear the vowel sounds in consonant-vowel-consonant (CVC) words.	Take off the initial or final letters to practise other word building activities.	Y1 T1 Word 1, 4	Writing: Spelling – Level A	AT2 Reading – Level 1 AT3 Writing – Level 1
page 26	Recognising rhyming words – 1	To recognise rhyming patterns of CVC and four-letter words.	After children have coloured in the picture look at the other CVC and four-letter word patterns.	Y1 T1 Word 1, 5, 6	Writing: Spelling – Level A	AT2 Reading – Level 1 AT3 Writing – Level 1
page 27	Recognising rhyming words – 2	To recognise rhyming patterns of CVC and four-letter words.	Highlight how the rhyming words along the path all end with 'old'. The children could make a poem using the words.	Y1 T1 Word 1, 5, 6	Writing: Spelling – Level A	AT2 Reading – Level 1 AT3 Writing – Level 1
page 28	Chips or ships?	To recognise objects that start with the initial consonant clusters.	This is a game. Explain to children that they have to keep going round the circle until one player has ten cubes.	Y1 T2 Word 3, Text 13	Writing: Spelling – Level A/B	AT2 Reading – Level 1 AT3 Writing – Level 1

NO FUSS

SCHOLASTIC
www.scholastic.co.uk

Page	Activity	Objective	Teachers' notes	National Literacy Strategy links	Scottish Curriculum links	KS1 Levels
page 29	Thank you	To recognise words using the initial consonant 'th'.	Read the letter with children and highlight the 'th' sound in the words. Look at the way the letter is set out and highlight the conventions used in letter writing. Spot clues in the letter to suggest what Aunt Thora sent.	Y1 T2 Word 3	Writing: Spelling – Level A/B	AT2 Reading – Level 1 AT3 Writing – Level 1
page 30	What a noise!	To recognise and use the initial consonant cluster 'wh'.	Ask the children about the characters using why, what, when and where questions.	Y1 T2 Word 3	Writing: Spelling – Level A/B	AT2 Reading – Level 1 AT3 Writing – Level 1
page 31	Find the blends	To recognise objects that start with the initial consonant clusters 'pl', 'ch', 'cl', 'dr', 'tr', 'fl', 'sh', 'st', 'gl' and 'sc'.	This activity can be used as an assessment to see how well children recognise different blends.	Y1 T2 Word 3	Writing: Spelling – Level A/B	AT2 Reading – Level 1 AT3 Writing – Level 1
page 32	Snail trail	To recognise the 'ai' pattern within words.	Ask the children to listen for the 'ai' sound in the title words and discuss the picture. When they draw their own snail trails make sure they are using 'ai' words.	Y1 T3 Word 1, 5	Writing: Spelling – Level A/B	AT2 Reading – Level 1 AT3 Writing – Level 1
page 33	Tell me….	To recognise the 'ea' pattern within words.	Make sure children understand the activity before they use the cards. Encourage a range of responses to the 'ea' questions.	Y1 T3 Word 5	Writing: Spelling – Level A/B	AT2 Reading – Level 1 AT3 Writing – Level 1
page 34	Toad and Goat	To recognise the 'oa' pattern within words.	Highlight the use of 'oa' in the title words. Ask children to think of another title using 'oa'.	Y1 T3 Word 1, 5;T2 Text 10	Writing: Spelling – Level A/B; Imaginative writing – Level A/B	AT2 Reading – Level 1 AT3 Writing – Level 1
page 35	Two of a kind?	To recognise the 'ee' and 'oo' patterns within words.	Before children start the activity, check they understand the terms 'consonant' and 'vowel'.	Y2 T1 Word 8	Writing: Spelling – Level A/B	AT2 Reading – Level 1 AT3 Writing – Level 1
page 36	Animal fun	To recognise final letter sounds for CVC words.	The children need to fill in the final letter for the CVC words before they can complete the acrostic puzzle. They solve the puzzle by writing the words across and then reading the letters downwards to find the cat's name.	Y1 T1 Word 3	Writing: Spelling – Level A/B	AT2 Reading – Level 1 AT3 Writing – Level 1
page 37	New clothes	To recognise different words that end with 's'.	Help the children to identify the animals and listen for the 's' ending. Remind them of words like 'is', 'was' and 'this' to help with story-telling.	Y1 T2 Word 8;T3 Text 14 Y2 T1 Word 7	Writing: Spelling – Level A/B; Imaginative writing – Level A/B	AT2 Reading – Level 1/2 AT3 Writing – Level 1/2
page 38	Going into the past	To investigate how the regular past tense works by adding 'ed' to the ends of words.	Ask children to read the activity carefully as some of the 'ed' spellings need some thought.	Y1 T3 Word 6 Y2 T1 Word 7	Writing: Spelling – Level A/B	AT2 Reading – Level 1/2 AT3 Writing – Level 1/2
page 39	My favourite -ing words	To investigate how words change by adding 'ing' to the end and to use present tense.	Have a display of 'ing' words that describe the different things the children like to do. The children should be aware that some words have certain rules for adding 'ing', such as words that drop a final 'e' or double their last letter.	Y1 T3 Word 6, Text 20 Y2 T1 Word 7	Writing: Spelling – Level A/B	AT2 Reading – Level 1/2 AT3 Writing – Level 1/2
pages 40 and 41	In the playground: 1 and 2	To investigate words that have the magic 'e' sound at the end.	Ask children to listen for long vowel sounds as they make new words in the wheel. Add more 'magic e' words to the picture, for example, rake, tube, hole, stone, lake, cone.	Y2 T1 Word 9	Writing: Spelling – Level A/B	AT2 Reading – Level 1/2 AT3 Writing – Level 1/2
page 42	Spell it to music	To make up words using a set number of letters and to put them in alphabetical order.	Highlight the different letter patterns that can be used in this activity. Challenge children to find the longest word out of the letters.	Y1 T1 Word 10;T2 Word 7	Writing: Spelling – Level A/B	AT2 Reading – Level 1/2 AT3 Writing – Level 1/2

Page	Activity	Objective	Teachers' notes	National Literacy Strategy links	Scottish Curriculum links	KS1 Levels
page 43	A jumbo muddle	To find words within words.	Use this activity for more able children. Encourage them to think of the different letter combinations that could be used to form new words.	Y1 T1 Word 10;T2 Word 7	Writing: Spelling – Level A/B	AT2 Reading – Level 1/2 AT3 Writing – Level 1/2
page 44	Picture sums	To show how two words can be put together to make a new word.	Let children experiment with different word combinations on a piece of paper until they get the correct compound words. Answers: horseshoe; milkman; football; candlestick; sheepdog; cowboy; jellyfish; houseboat.	Y2 T2 Word 4	Writing: Spelling – Level A/B/C	AT2 Reading – Level 1/2 AT3 Writing – Level 1/2
page 45	Take your partner	To make compound words out of two words.	Children could trace over the shape and write in their own compound words for a partner to solve. Answers: armchair; birthday; cannot; policeman; inside; grandmother; pigsty; bedroom.	Y2 T2 Word 4	Writing: Spelling – Level A/B/C	AT2 Reading – Level 1/2 AT3 Writing – Level 1/2
page 46	Homophones	To understand the term 'homophone' and recognise homophones.	This activity can be played by two or three children. After the activity ask children to collect more homophone words.	Y2 T1 Word 4; T3 Word 6	Writing: Spelling – Level A/B/C	AT2 Reading – Level 1/2 AT3 Writing – Level 1/2
page 47	Sounds like…	To investigate words that sound alike (homophones).	Homophones are words that sound the same but have different meanings and usually different spellings. Highlight the fact that there are alternative ways of spelling the same sound.	Y2 T1 Word 4; T3 Word 6	Writing: Spelling – Level A/B/C	AT2 Reading – Level 1/2 AT3 Writing – Level 1/2
page 48	Opposite sides – opposite words	To recognise and investigate the opposite meanings of words.	Let children know that the term for describing the opposite meaning of a word is an antonym.	Y2 T2 Word 11	Writing: Spelling – Level A/B/C	AT2 Reading – Level 1/2 AT3 Writing – Level 1/2
page 49	In other words	To understand the term 'synonyms' and collect words for four examples.	Show children how to use a thesaurus before the activity. Ask them to choose a few more words and their synonyms.	Y2 T3 Word 10	Writing: Spelling – Level A/B/C	AT2 Reading – Level 1/2 AT3 Writing – Level 1/2
page 50	Mehndi patterns	To encourage the correct letter formation of curves.	Highlight that the patterns must be drawn from left to right. It is important to ask for parent's permission first. You will need Henna powder for this activity. Display the finished patterns.	Y1 T1 Word 13, 14	Writing: Handwriting – Level A	AT3 Writing – Level 1
page 51	Knitting with Mrs Mopple	To encourage the correct letter formation of loops.	Children may want to use different coloured pencils to make the knitting pattern colourful.	Y1 T1 Word 13, 14	Writing: Handwriting – Level A	AT3 Writing – Level 1
page 52	Aliens	To encourage the drawing of straight and diagonal lines.	Children need to take their time when completing this picture. Highlight the need of a ruler when they design their own alien.	Y1 T1 Word 13, 14	Writing: Handwriting – Level A	AT3 Writing – Level 1
page 53	Umbrella pattern	To make patterns using a mix of lines, curves and circles.	This is a good re-enforcement activity to practise the different patterns.	Y1 T1 Word 13, 14	Writing: Handwriting – Level A	AT3 Writing – Level 1
page 54	Feed the caterpillar	To practise forming the letters 'i', 'j', 'l', 't', 'u' and 'y'.	Children should start where the dot is and try not to take their pencil off the letter until the end.	Y1 T1 Word 14; T2 Word 11; T3 Word 10	Writing: Handwriting – Level A/B	AT3 Writing – Level 1/2
page 55	Beautiful butterfly	To practise forming the letters 'b', 'h', 'n', 'p' and 'r'.	Children should go over the letters at the top of the page before they decorate the butterfly wings.	Y1 T1 Word 14; T2 Word 11; T3 Word 10	Writing: Handwriting – Level A/B	AT3 Writing – Level 1/2
page 56	Quilt covers	To practise forming the letters 'v', 'w', 'x' and 'z'.	Make sure children complete the started quilts before they do their own designs. Ask them to identify which letter shapes are used in the designs.	Y1 T1 Word 14; T2 Word 11; T3 Word 10	Writing: Handwriting – Level A/B	AT3 Writing – Level 1/2

■SCHOLASTIC
www.scholastic.co.uk

Page	Activity	Objective	Teachers' notes	National Literacy Strategy links	Scottish Curriculum links	KS1 Levels
page 57	Party time	To practise forming the letters 'c', 'o', 'a', 'd', 'g', 'q' and 'e'.	Children should practise the letters at the top of the page before they design their wrapping paper. Encourage them to use all the letters in their design.	Y1 T1 Word 14; T2 Word 11; T3 Word 10	Writing: Handwriting – Level A/B	AT3 Writing – Level 1/2
page 58	Peacock feathers	To practise forming the letter 'f'.	Highlight how the letter 'f' is formed in two movements. Use coloured pencils to decorate the feathers with the letter 'f'.	Y1 T1 Word 14; T2 Word 11; T3 Word 10	Writing: Handwriting – Level A/B	AT3 Writing – Level 1/2
page 59	Special k/k	To practise forming the letter 'k/k'.	Highlight how the letter 'k' can be written in two ways.	Y1 T1 Word 14; T2 Word 11; T3 Word 10	Writing: Handwriting – Level A/B	AT3 Writing – Level 1/2
page 60	Hisssss!	To practise forming the letter 's'.	Let children experiment with the different ways of writing the letter 's'. Do they prefer one method over another?	Y1 T1 Word 14; T2 Word 11; T3 Word 10	Writing: Handwriting – Level A/B	AT3 Writing – Level 1/2
page 61	Sign here!	To practise forming and writing capital letters.	Let children make large signs using capital letters for a display.	Y1 T1 Word 13, Text 16; T2 Word 11; T3 Word 10	Writing: Handwriting – Level A/B; Functional writing – Level A/B	AT3 Writing – Level 1/2
page 62	Placemats	To practise forming two-letter words using diagonal joins.	Children should trace their finger over the letters to see how they are formed before writing the words.	Y2 T1 Word 11, 12; T2 Word 14; T3 Word 12	Writing: Handwriting – Level A/B	AT3 Writing – Level 1/2/3
page 63	Curtains	To practise forming two-letter words using horizontal joins.	Highlight how the letters are joined with a horizontal line.	Y2 T1 Word 11, 12; T2 Word 14; T3 Word 12	Writing: Handwriting – Level A/B/C	AT3 Writing – Level 1/2/3
page 64	Build a sentence – journeys	To match and build sentences.	Each sentence has a pattern of a subject, verb and object which helps children to construct their own sentences.	Y1 T1 Sentence 1, 4, 6	Writing: Functional, Personal and Imaginative writing – Level A/B/C; Reading: Reading for enjoyment – Level A/B/C	AT2 Reading – Level 1/2; AT3 Writing – Level 1/2
page 65	A train journey	To build simple sentences.	Children may need help in cutting and making the train.	Y1 T1 Sentence 1, 4, 6; T2 Sentence 3	Writing: Functional, Personal and Imaginative writing – Level A/B/C; Reading: Reading for enjoyment – Level A/B/C	AT2 Reading – Level 2; AT3 Writing – Level 2
page 66	Off we go on the train	To predict and add words into simple sentences.	Talk through the sheet with the children, looking at the pictures and reading the words.	Y1 T2 Sentence 2, 3; T3 Sentence 3, 4	Writing: Functional, Personal and Imaginative writing – Level A/B/C; Reading: Reading for enjoyment – Level A/B/C	AT2 Reading – Level 2/3; AT3 Writing – Level 2/3
page 67	Missing words	To predict and place words into sentences.	Encourage children to read the text through before deciding on the correct missing words. This activity employs cloze and sequencing techniques to extend the children's understanding of language structure.	Y1 T2 Text 14; T3 Sentence 4	Writing: Functional, Personal and Imaginative writing – Level A/B/C; Reading: Reading for enjoyment – Level A/B/C	AT2 Reading – Level 2; AT3 Writing – Level 2
page 68	All mixed up	To re-order sentences.	Highlight how capital letters and full stops give clues to the correct sentence structure. The completed story derives its humour from wordplay, encouraging an interest in words and their use and interpretation in different contexts.	Y1 T3 Sentence 4	Writing: Functional, Personal and Imaginative writing – Level A/B/C; Reading: Reading for enjoyment – Level A/B/C	AT2 Reading – Level 2/3; AT3 Writing – Level 2/3
page 69	Name the object!	To introduce the concept of what is a noun.	For less able children, write down the nouns with them and let them write the first letter in the labels.	Y2 T2 Sentence 4; T3 Sentence 2	Writing: Functional, Personal and Imaginative writing – Level A/B/C	AT3 Writing – Level 2

Page	Activity	Objective	Teachers' notes	National Literacy Strategy links	Scottish Curriculum links	KS1 Levels
page 70	Word inventions	To investigate nouns and their function.	Discuss how the first of the two nouns in the pairs serves the same function as an adjective by describing the second noun. A cake tree is a tree that grows cakes; in the same way an apple tree grows apples!	Y2 T2 Word 5, Sentence 4;T3 Sentence 2	Reading: Reading for enjoyment – Level A/B/C	AT2 Reading – Level 2
page 71	What are they doing?	To introduce the concept of a verb.	This activity supports the idea of what a verb is. Ask the children for more examples of verbs.	Y2 T2 Sentence 4, 5;T3 Sentence 2, 3	Writing: Functional, Personal and Imaginative writing – Level A/B/C; Reading: Reading for enjoyment – Level A/B/C	AT2 Reading – Level 2 / AT3 Writing – Level 2
page 72	In the future	To recognise the use of the future tense of verbs.	Ask children to identify the three ways in which future tense is indicated: *shall, will,* and *going to.*	Y2 T2 Sentence 4, 5;T3 Sentence 2, 3	Writing: Functional, Personal and Imaginative writing – Level A/B/C; Reading: Reading for enjoyment – Level A/B/C	AT2 Reading – Level 2/3 / AT3 Writing – Level 2/3
page 73	What did you do?	To recognise the use of the past tense of verbs.	Highlight the use of 'ed' at the end of words to indicate the past.	Y2 T2 Sentence 4, 5;T3 Sentence 2, 3 Text 10	Writing: Functional, Personal and Imaginative writing – Level A/B/C; Reading: Reading for enjoyment – Level A/B/C	AT2 Reading – Level 2/3 / AT3 Writing – Level 2/3
page 74	Who did what?	To recognise pronouns and their use.	This activity challenges children to choose the pronoun to replace given nouns.	Y2 T2 Sentence 4; T3 Sentence 2	Writing: Functional, Personal and Imaginative writing – Level A/B/C; Reading: Reading for enjoyment – Level A/B/C	AT2 Reading – Level 2/3 / AT3 Writing – Level 2/3
page 75	He, she, it	To recognise pronouns and their use.	In this activity children have to first identify pronouns, then replace given nouns with pronouns and, finally, to supply pronouns to fill gaps in sentences.	Y2 T2 Sentence 4; T3 Sentence 2	Writing: Functional, Personal and Imaginative writing – Level A/B/C; Reading: Reading for enjoyment – Level A/B/C	AT2 Reading – Level 2/3 / AT3 Writing – Level 2/3
page 76	A dragon in the playground	To use nouns, verbs and adjectives to produce an interesting story.	Look at the pictures and read through the words before the children start writing their stories. Remind the children that stories should have a beginning, middle and an end.	Y2 T2 Sentence 4, 5, Text 13;T3 Sentence 2, 3	Writing: Functional, Personal and Imaginative writing – Level A/B/C; Reading: Reading for enjoyment – Level A/B/C	AT2 Reading – Level 2/3 / AT3 Writing – Level 2/3
page 77	Name it	To recognise that capital letters are used at the beginning of proper names.	As an extension to this activity, ask the children to collect and write down the names of the roads they live on.	Y1 T2 Sentence 4; T3 Sentence 5 / Y2 T1 Sentence 5	Writing: Punctuation and structure – Level A/B; Knowledge about language – Level B; Reading: Reading for information and enjoyment – Level A/B	AT2 Reading – Level 2 / AT3 Writing – Level 2
page 78	Riddle muddle	To recognise a question and add in a question mark.	The children must match up the riddles and answers and add the question marks where appropriate.	Y1 T3 Sentence 7 / Y2 T3 Sentence 7, Text 8, 11	Writing: Punctuation and structure – Level A/B/C; Knowledge about language – Level B/C; Reading: Reading for information and enjoyment – Level A/B/C	AT2 Reading – Level 2/3 / AT3 Writing – Level 2/3
page 79	Guess the questions	To write questions.	Children must read the answers first and think of interview-style questions to match them. This activity reinforces an understanding of the question and answer format.	Y1 T3 Sentence 7 / Y2 T3 Sentence 6, 7	Writing: Punctuation and structure – Level A/B/C; Knowledge about language – Level B/C; Reading: Reading for information and enjoyment – Level A/B/C	AT2 Reading – Level 2 / AT3 Writing – Level 2
page 80	Take a break!	To use commas in lists.	Children can write out their own fun lists using commas, using the given model as a starting point.	Y1 T2 Text 25 / Y2 T1 Sentence 3; T2 Sentence 8	Writing: Punctuation and structure – Level A/B/C; Knowledge about language – Level B/C; Reading: Reading for information and enjoyment – Level A/B/C	AT2 Reading – Level 2/3 / AT3 Writing – Level 2/3
page 81	Watching television – what are they saying?	To write text in speech bubbles.	This activity develops an understanding of direct speech. Ask the children to write a cartoon with speech bubbles of what happened next. Remind them that they should only write the actual words spoken in the speech bubbles.	Y1 T2 Text 4 / Y2 T2 Sentence 7	Writing: Punctuation and structure – Level A/B/C; Knowledge about language – Level B/C	AT3 Writing – Level 2/3

SCHOLASTIC
www.scholastic.co.uk

Page	Activity	Objective	Teachers' notes	National Literacy Strategy links	Scottish Curriculum links	KS1 Levels
page 82	What are they saying?	To match the dialogue to the correct speech bubble.	Children have to re-order the sentences before they write them in the correct speech bubble. They should understand that changing the order of the words could change the meaning of the sentence. Use the capital letters and punctuation marks as clues to determine the first and last words of the sentences.	Y1 T2 Text 4 Y2 T2 Sentence 7	Writing: Punctuation and structure – Level A/B/C; Knowledge about language – Level B/C Reading: Reading for information and enjoyment – Level A/B/C	AT2 Reading – Level 2/3; AT3 Writing – Level 2/3
page 83	Make a new rhyme	To write a simple rhyme using patterns as cues.	Children need to look at the pictures and read out the rhymes to help them choose the right words.	Y1 T1 Text 2, 6, 10; T2 Text 2, 11, 13; T3 Text 2, 9, 15	Writing: Imaginative writing – Level A Reading: Reading for enjoyment and Reading aloud – Level A	AT1 Speaking and listening – Level 1/2 AT2 Reading – Level 1/2 AT3 Writing – Level 2
page 84	My lunch box	To put a picture story into the correct sequence.	Ask the children to talk about what is happening in the pictures and to recount the story.	Y1 T1 Text 5, 11; T2 Text 4, 7, 10, 14; T3 Text 5	Writing: Imaginative writing – Level A Reading: Reading for enjoyment and Reading aloud – Level A	AT1 Speaking and listening – Level 1/2 AT2 Reading – Level 1/2
page 85	Completing stories – the big puddle	To add dialogue to complete a story.	Children need to look through all the text before deciding where the extracts of direct speech should be placed. Highlight how direct speech is presented in written form using speech marks.	Y1 T2 Text 4; T3 Sentence 4, Text 3, 5 Y2 T1 Text 4, 5; T2 Sentence 6	Writing: Imaginative writing – Level A/B Reading: Reading for enjoyment and Reading aloud – Level A/B	AT1 Speaking and listening – Level 1/2 AT2 Reading – Level 1/2 AT3 Writing – Level 2
page 86	The wind and the sun	To put a story into the correct sequence.	When children have completed the story, ask them to highlight the first and last paragraphs of the story.	Y2 T1 Text 4,5	Reading: Reading for enjoyment and Reading aloud – Level A/B	AT2 Reading – Level 2/3
page 87	Picture story writing – the caves	To write a story with given setting, characters and plot.	Children need to read through the given text first and then complete the story using clear short sentences.	Y2 T1 Text 4, 5; T2 Text 4, 13;	Writing: Imaginative writing and Knowledge about language – Level A/B Reading: Reading for enjoyment and Reading aloud – Level A/B	AT2 Reading – Level 2/3 AT3 Writing – Level 2
page 88	Language map	To notice the difference between spoken and written forms.	The language map is a useful device for focusing the children's attention on the language they hear spoken in order to compare language in different contexts. Children could use their language maps to write a short story or comic strip.	Y1 T1 Text 3; T2 Text 4; T3 Text 3; T1-3 Word – vocabulary extension	Talking: Conveying information, instructions and directions – Level A/B Listening: Listening for information, instructions and directions – Level A/B Reading: Knowledge about language – Level B Writing: Knowledge about language – Level B	AT1 Speaking and listening – Level 1/2/3 AT2 Reading – Level 2/3 AT3 Writing – Level 2/3
page 89	What would you like?	To notice the difference between spoken and written forms.	Children could play a game where they take down food orders from each other. This activity gives further practise in noticing the difference between spoken and written English.	Y1 T3 Sentence 4 Y2 T1 Text 3, 15	Talking: Conveying information, instructions and directions – Level A/B Listening: Listening for information, instructions and directions – Level A/B Reading: Knowledge about language – Level B Writing: Knowledge about language – Level B	AT1 Speaking and listening – Level 2/3 AT2 Reading – Level 2/3 AT3 Writing – Level 2/3
page 90	Different story types	To investigate different story genres.	Discuss a genre children know well, looking at characters, places and events. It may also be helpful to show them book covers that illustrate different story types.	Y1 T2 Text 6 Y2 T2 Text 3	Reading: Awareness of genre – Level A/B/C	AT2 Reading – Level 2
page 91	Choose-your-own fairy story	To investigate features of fairy tales.	The children need to look at the words and pictures to decide how they would like to invent their own story. They can colour in the pictures that they would like to use in their story. Encourage children to continue their stories using words and pictures.	Y1 T2 Text 5, 6, 10; T3 Text 5, 6	Reading: Reading for enjoyment and Awareness of genre – Level A/B/C Writing: Imaginative writing – Level A/B/C	AT2 Reading – Level 1/2 AT3 Writing – Level 2

Page	Activity	Objective	Teachers' notes	National Literacy Strategy links	Scottish Curriculum links	KS1 Levels
page 92	Identikit pictures	To describe a character.	Children need to concentrate on the details of their characters when writing the descriptions.	Y1 T2 Text 8, 15 Y2 T2 Text 6, 14	Writing: Functional writing – Level A/B Reading: Reading for information – Level A/B	AT2 Reading – Level 2/3 AT3 Writing – Level 2/3
page 93	How do they feel!	To describe the feelings of different characters.	Discuss any similar situations in which the children may have been involved.	Y1 T2 Text 8, 15 Y2 T2 Text 6, 14	Writing: Personal and Imaginative writing – Level A/B Reading: Reading for enjoyment – Level A/B	AT2 Reading – Level 2/3 AT3 Writing – Level 2/3
page 94	My monster	To produce a character profile of a monster.	Discuss monsters from other stories, including books and films. Talk about what they looked like and how they behaved.	Y1 T2 Text 8, 15 Y2 T2 Text 6, 14	Writing: Imaginative writing – Level A/B Reading: Reading for enjoyment – Level A/B	AT2 Reading – Level 2/3 AT3 Writing – Level 2/3
page 95	My monster story	To write a story about a monster.	This sheet can be used with the monster profile from 'My monster'. Make sure the children plan their story before they start writing. Draw their attention to the 'To think about' section on the sheet.	Y1 T2 Text 8 15 Y2 T2 Text 6, 14	Writing: Imaginative writing – Level A/B Reading: Reading for enjoyment – Level A/B	AT2 Reading – Level 2/3 AT3 Writing – Level 2/3
page 96	A story train	To investigate different fairy-tale story openings.	The train outline can be used to make openings for other story genres.	Y1 T2 Text 6, 10, 16	Writing: Imaginative writing and Knowledge about language – Level A/B Reading: Reading for enjoyment and Knowledge about language – Level A/B	AT2 Reading – Level 2/3 AT3 Writing – Level 2/3
page 97	Writing story openings	To investigate different ways of opening a story.	Show the children a picture of your choice and ask them to write four different story openings for it.	Y1 T2 Text 6 Y2 T2 Text 4	Writing: Imaginative writing and Knowledge about language – Level A/B Reading: Reading for enjoyment and Knowledge about language – Level A/B	AT2 Reading – Level 1/2 AT3 Writing – Level 2
page 98	Chain of events	To recognise how stories can be based around a series of events.	Before the activity, choose a known story and highlight its main events. Explain that many stories are based around a series of related events.	Y1 T2 Text 7,14 Y2 T1 Text 4, 5, 10	Writing: Imaginative writing and Knowledge about language – Level A/B Reading: Reading for enjoyment and Knowledge about language – Level A/B	AT2 Reading – Level 2/3 AT3 Writing – Level 2/3
page 99	Writing story endings	To investigate different ways of ending a story.	Discuss where each picture is set, what is happening, who the main character is and so on before the children write their story endings. Talk about the endings of stories known to the children. Ask them which type of endings they prefer and the reasons for their choice.	Y1 T2 Text 8 15 Y2 T2 Text 6, 14	Writing: Imaginative writing and Knowledge about language – Level A/B Reading: Reading for enjoyment and Knowledge about language – Level A/B	AT2 Reading – Level 2/3 AT3 Writing – Level 2/3
page 100	Describing the seaside	To describe a specific place.	Discuss the seaside with the children. Use pictures, videos or sound effects to establish a sense of the place.	Y1 T1 Text 5 Y2 T2 Text 13	Writing: Imaginative writing and Knowledge about language – Level A/B Reading: Reading for enjoyment and Knowledge about language – Level A/B	AT3 Writing – Level 1/2/3
page 101	Describing the setting	To describe different settings in detail.	Use this sheet to encourage the children to establish different settings for their writing.	Y1 T1 Text 5 Y2 T2 Text 13	Writing: Imaginative writing and Knowledge about language – Level A/B Reading: Reading for enjoyment and Knowledge about language – Level A/B	AT3 Writing – Level 1/2/3
page 102	Making fairy stories modern	To recognise and adapt the conventions of a traditional tale.	Ask children for suggestions about how the fairy tale conventions can be changed to make them 'modern'. Extend the children by encouraging them to change as many aspects of the story as they can.	Y1 T2 Text 14, 16 Y2 T2 Text 13	Writing: Imaginative writing and Knowledge about language – Level A/B/C Reading: Reading for enjoyment, Awareness of genre and Knowledge about language – Level A/B/C	AT2 Reading – Level 2/3 AT3 Writing – Level 2/3

SCHOLASTIC
www.scholastic.co.uk

Page	Activity	Objective	Teachers' notes	National Literacy Strategy links	Scottish Curriculum links	KS1 Levels
page 103	Guess who puzzles	To recognise and understand riddles.	Encourage children to write their own animal riddles and make a class collection. Answers: elephant; cockerel; squirrel; dog.	Y2 T3 Text 8, 11	Writing: Imaginative writing and Knowledge about language – Level A/B/C Reading: Reading for enjoyment, Awareness of genre and Knowledge about language – Level A/B/C	AT2 Reading – Level 2/3 AT3 Writing – Level 2/3
page 104	Alliteration	To understand the term 'alliteration' and to use alliteration for writing.	This sheet can also be used as a group or class activity.	Y2 T3 Text 8, 11	Writing: Imaginative writing and Knowledge about language – Level A/B/C Reading: Reading for enjoyment, Awareness of genre and Knowledge about language – Level A/B/C	AT2 Reading – Level 2/3 AT3 Writing – Level 2/3
page 105	Tongue-twister	To recognise and understand the use of tongue twisters.	Highlight that this activity uses alliterative words. Try other letters or an alliterative sentence.	Y2 T3 Text 8, 11	Writing: Imaginative writing and Knowledge about language – Level A/B/C Reading: Reading for enjoyment, Awareness of genre and Knowledge about language – Level A/B/C	AT2 Reading – Level 2/3 AT3 Writing – Level 2/3
page 106	At the airport	To read and understand the use of signs.	Ask children to think of other signs they have seen in their local area and why they are needed.	Y1 T1 Sentence 4, Text 12, 14; T2 Text 23	Writing: Functional writing – Level A/B Reading: Reading for information – Level A/B	AT2 Reading – Level 1/2 AT3 Writing – Level 2
page 107	Wet! Wet! Wet!	To write simple captions.	Highlight how captions are written in short sentences. This sheet provides an opportunity for children to talk about verbs.	Y1 T1 Sentence 4, Text 12, 14; T2 Text 23	Writing: Functional writing – Level A/B Reading: Reading for information – Level A/B	AT3 Writing – Level 2
page 108	Do you know the parts of a flower?	To write simple labels for a drawing of a plant.	Ask the children to look for examples of labels around the classroom and their uses.	Y1 T2 Text 22	Writing: Functional writing – Level A/B Reading: Reading for information – Level A/B	AT2 Reading – Level 1/2 AT3 Writing – Level 2
page 109	A Roman soldier	To label a picture using given information.	Use a highlighter pen to show children how to find the information needed for labelling.	Y1 T3 Text 19, 21	Writing: Functional writing – Level A/B Reading: Reading for information – Level A/B	AT2 Reading – Level 2/3 AT3 Writing – Level 2/3
page 110	The giant's list	To write a list.	Before starting the activity, discuss different lists and why we use them.	Y1 T1 Text 13, 15	Writing: Functional writing – Level A/B Reading: Reading for information – Level A/B	AT2 Reading – Level 2/3 AT3 Writing – Level 2/3
page 111	School rules	To write a list of four school rules.	Highlight how we can make lists to sort out important information such as rules. Discuss what rules are and why they are needed.	Y1 T3 Text 22 Y2 T1 Text 14, 16	Writing: Functional writing – Level A/B Reading: Reading for information – Level A/B	AT2 Reading – Level 2/3 AT3 Writing – Level 2/3
page 112	Design a robot	To listen and follow simple instructions.	Children should work in pairs for this activity, sitting back to back, each with a copy of the sheet. They should take turns directing each other to build a robot.	Y1 T1 Text 13	Talking: Conveying information, instructions and directions – Level A/B Listening: Listening for information, instructions and directions – Level A/B	AT1 Speaking and listening – Level 1/2
page 113	Spiral adventure	To write rules for a board game.	This activity allows children to understand the features of rule-writing by writing their own rules for a board game.	Y2 T1 Text 13, 14, 15, 16, 18	Writing: Functional writing – Level A/B Reading: Reading for information – Level A/B	AT2 Reading – Level 2/3 AT3 Writing – Level 2/3
page 114	The alien planet	To recognise positional words used for directions.	Play simple activity games in which children can practise positional language such as *Sit under your chair*.	Y1 T1 Text 13, 16; T3 Sentence 4 Y2 T1 Text 13, 14,	Talking: Conveying information, instructions and directions – Level A/B Listening: Listening for information, instructions and directions – Level A/B Reading: Reading for information – Level A/B	AT1 Speaking and listening – Level 1/2 AT2 Reading – Level 1/2

Page	Activity	Objective	Teachers' notes	National Literacy Strategy links	Scottish Curriculum links	KS1 Levels
page 115	Compass directions	To listen and follow directions.	Children should work in pairs for this activity, sitting back to back, each with a copy of the sheet. They should take turns directing each other using simple points of the compass and descriptive language.	Y1 T1 Text 13 Y2 T1 Text 13	Talking: Conveying information, instructions and directions – Level A/B Listening: Listening for information, instructions and directions – Level A/B	AT1 Speaking and listening – Level 1/2
page 116	Fact and fiction	To understand the difference between fact and fiction.	Let children visit the school or local library to collect examples of fact and fiction books to identify the differences and develop an understanding of their features.	Y1 T2 Text 17,18, 19, 25; T3 Text 17, 20, 21 Y2 T3 Text 13, 20	Writing: Functional and Imaginative writing – Level A/B/C Reading: Reading for information and enjoyment and Awareness of genre – Level A/B/C	AT2 Reading – Level 2/3 AT3 Writing – Level 2/3
page 117	Pen-friend from outer space	To understand the features of letter writing.	Discuss the difference between an informal letter and formal letter. This activity gives children the opportunity to use adjectives and adverbs, and to link sentences coherently.	Y1 T3 Text 20	Writing: Imaginative writing – Level A/B Reading: Awareness of genre – Level A/B	AT2 Reading – Level 2/3 AT3 Writing – Level 2/3
page 118	A postcard from a castle	To understand the features of writing a postcard.	Explain how postcards are divided into two sections, for writing the message and the address.	Y1 T3 Text 20	Writing: Imaginative writing – Level A/B Reading: Awareness of genre – Level A/B	AT2 Reading – Level 2/3 AT3 Writing – Level 2/3
page 119	Greetings!	To understand the features of writing cards.	Show children some greeting cards as points of reference. Encourage them to choose their own words for the greetings card.	Y1 T3 Text 20	Writing: Personal writing – Level A/B Reading: Awareness of genre and Knowledge about language – Level A/B	AT2 Reading – Level 2/3 AT3 Writing – Level 2/3
page 120	An unusual folding abc	To learn how to use a dictionary.	This activity is a good starting point for children to investigate how a dictionary is set out. As an extension, the children could write the meanings of some of the unusual words on the back of the page.	Y1 T2 Text 20, 21 Y2 T2 Text 16, 17, 20	Writing: Functional writing – Level A/B Reading: Awareness of genre and Knowledge about language – Level A/B	AT2 Reading – Level 2/3 AT3 Writing – Level 2/3
page 121	Reporting – the cycling accident	To learn how to write a simple report about an incident.	Encourage children to devise their own incidents and dramatise them. They could write their role-plays out afterwards.	Y1 T2 Text 25 Y1 T3 Text 18, 20	Writing: Functional writing – Level A/B Reading: Awareness of genre and Knowledge about language – Level A/B	AT2 Reading – Level 2/3 AT3 Writing – Level 2/3
page 122	Writing charts from text	To convert information into a simple text.	Get children to use a highlighter pen to highlight the information needed to fill in the chart.	Y1 T3 Text 19, 22 Y2 T2 Text 21	Writing: Functional writing – Level A/B/C Reading: Reading for information – Level A/B/C	AT2 Reading – Level 2/3 AT3 Writing – Level 2/3
page 123	Natural/ man-made materials	To sort information into a chart.	Go through the objects on the page with the children to discuss in which column they should be placed.	Y1 T3 Text 19, 22 Y2 T2 Text 21	Writing: Functional writing – Level A/B/C Reading: Reading for information – Level A/B/C	AT2 Reading – Level 2/3 AT3 Writing – Level 2/3
page 124	Finding out from charts	To read a simple chart and turn information into sentences.	After the activity, encourage children to produce another chart on a spider and butterfly.	Y1 T3 Text 19, 22	Writing: Functional writing – Level A/B/C Reading: Reading for information – Level A/B/C	AT2 Reading – Level 2/3 AT3 Writing – Level 2/3
page 125	Frogs	To use a flow chart or diagram in non-fiction.	Let the children look at other books about frogs before they start this activity. Emphasise that neat and concise writing is needed for this activity.	Y2 T2 Text 19, 21	Writing: Functional writing – Level A/B/C Reading: Reading for information – Level A/B/C	AT2 Reading – Level 2/3 AT3 Writing – Level 2/3
page 126	Read about the hedgehog	To learn how to read texts and extract important information.	Before starting the activity, show children how to use a highlighter pen to mark the vital information. Let them discuss which words are of importance.	Y2 T3 Text 16, 17, 18, 19, 20	Writing: Functional writing – Level A/B/C Reading: Reading for information – Level A/B/C	AT2 Reading – Level 2/3 AT3 Writing – Level 2/3
page 127	My spidergram	To write facts in an interesting way.	Children will need to carry out some research on spiders before they can write in the facts.	Y1 T3 Text 19, 22 Y2 T3 Text 14, 21	Writing: Functional writing – Level A/B/C Reading: Reading for information – Level A/B/C	AT2 Reading – Level 2/3 AT3 Writing – Level 2/3

SCHOLASTIC
www.scholastic.co.uk

A letter bird

This is a letter bird.

✤ Write down the letters which make up the letter bird.

There are eight:

_____

There are 26 letters in the alphabet:

A a B b C c D d E e F f G g H h I i J j K k L l M m

N n O o P p Q q R r S s T t U u V v W w X x Y y Z z

✤ Use the letters, either capitals or small letters or both, to draw a letter person or a letter animal.

✤ Choose one letter and turn it into something else.
For example **c** might become a caterpillar.

Alphabet Arthur

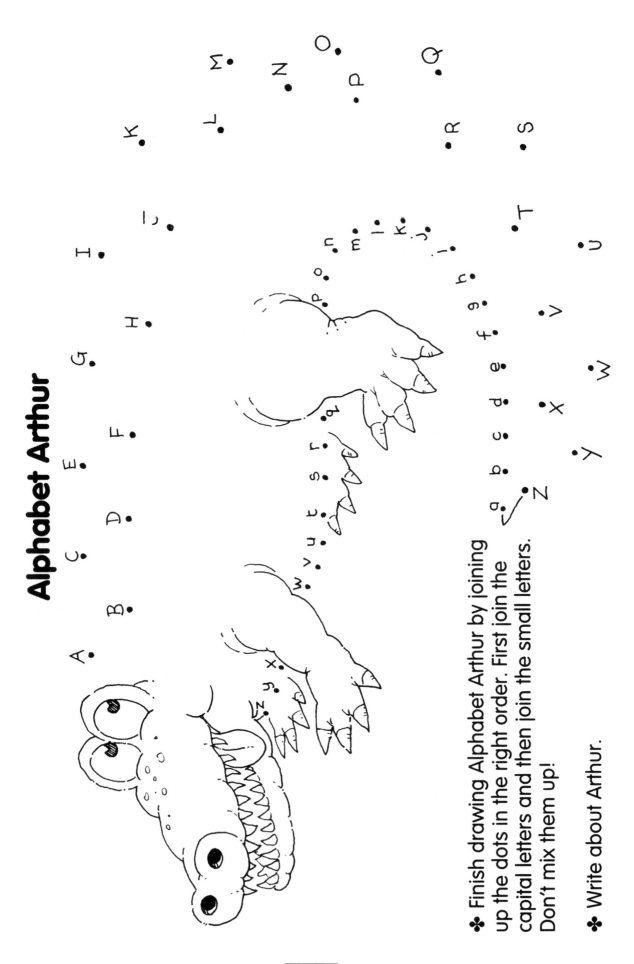

♣ Finish drawing Alphabet Arthur by joining up the dots in the right order. First join the capital letters and then join the small letters. Don't mix them up!

♣ Write about Arthur.

SCHOLASTIC
www.scholastic.co.uk

Name _____

✿ Pink butterfly

✿ Write **b** or **p** at the beginning of each word.

✿ Colour all the **p** shapes pink.

✿ Choose another colour for the **b** shapes.

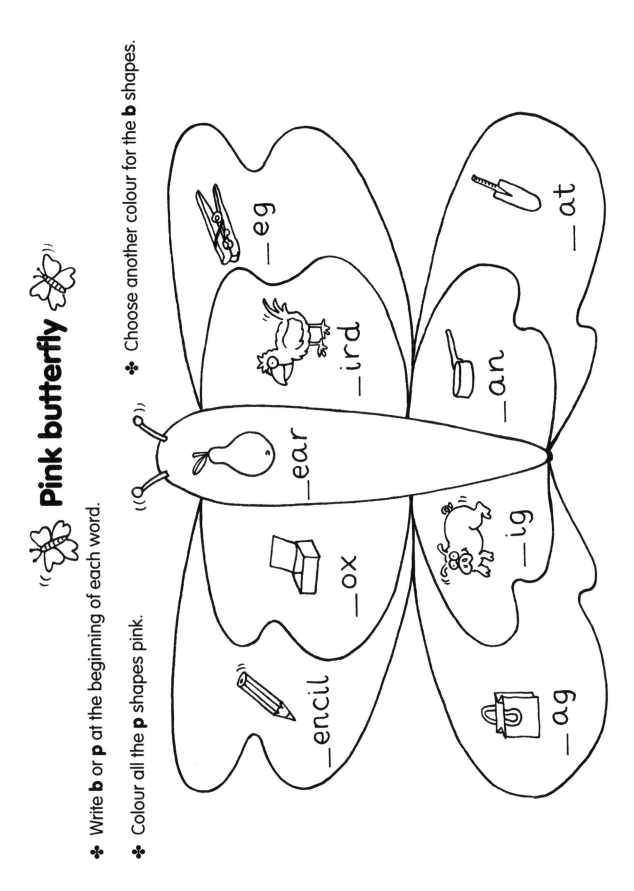

—eg

—ird

—at

—an

—ear

—ox

—ig

—encil

—ag

Carl the cat

✤ Colour all the shapes that have a picture of an object starting with **c** in them.

✤ Cut out the coloured shapes.

✤ Can you pin/stick them together to make **C**arl the **c**at?
You could attach the shapes using paper-fasteners.

■SCHOLASTIC
www.scholastic.co.uk

Can you find Tom?

❖ Find the shapes that have pictures starting with **d** in them. Colour them red.

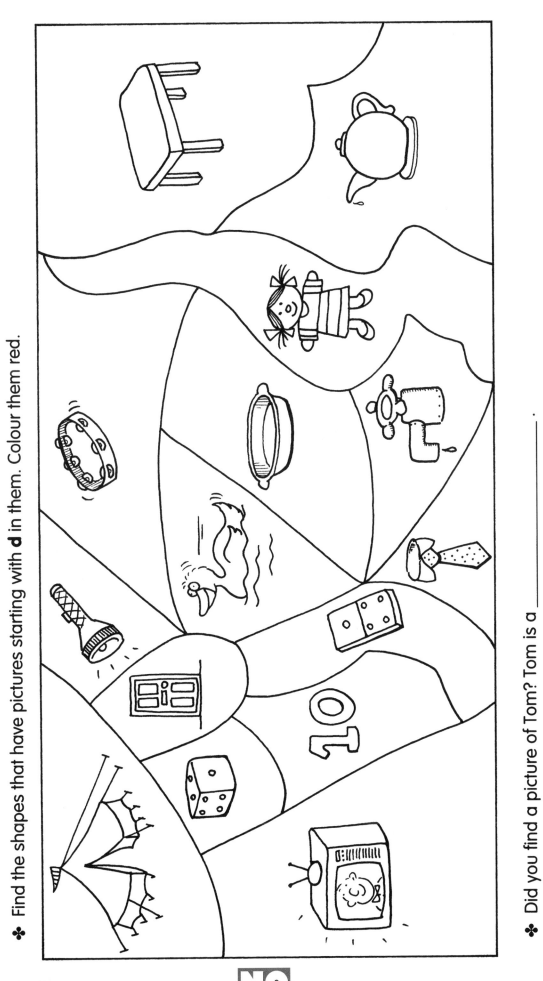

❖ Did you find a picture of Tom? Tom is a _____

Moving day

Fatima and **Val** are moving house.

❖ Write **f** or **v** at the beginning of each word.

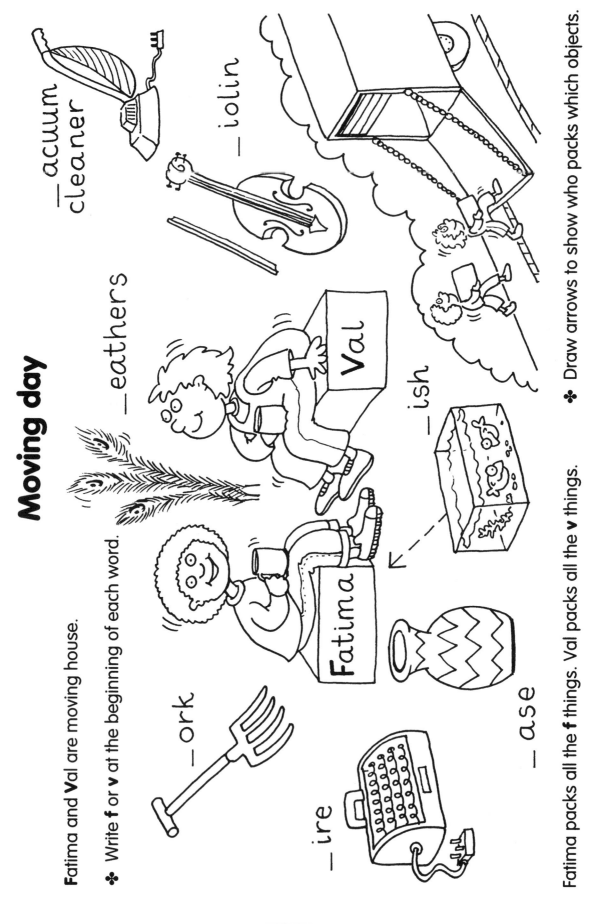

_acuum cleaner

_iolin

_eathers

_ish

_ase

_ork

_ire

Val

Fatima

❖ Fatima packs all the **f** things. Val packs all the **v** things.

❖ Draw arrows to show who packs which objects.

Name _____

Sort the toys

✤ Can you help Hardeep sort out his toys? Name the toys and write **h**, **j** or **m** next to each picture.

✤ Now cut out the toys and stick them on their proper shelves.

Name _____

Robot's walk

Take **R**odney **R**obot to see **R**abbit.

✤ Can you name the pictures on the track below? Follow the paths where the pictures begin with **r**.

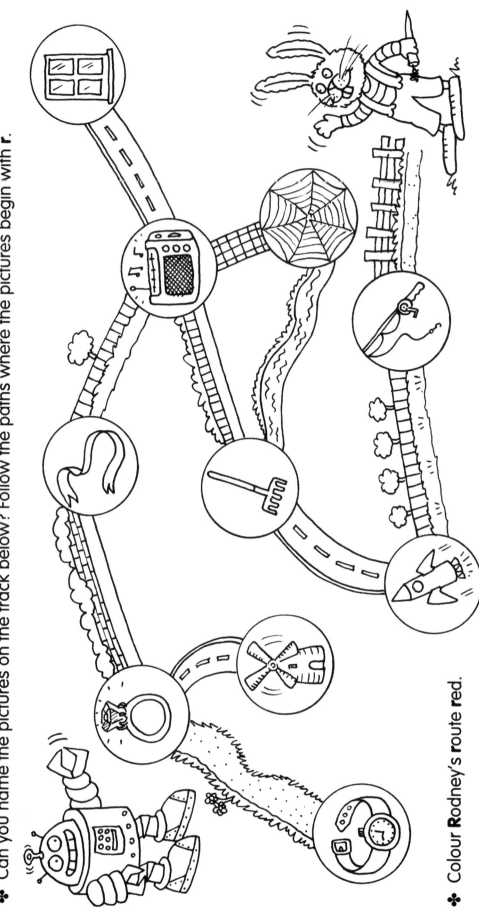

✤ Colour **R**odney's route red.

What's my name?

❖ Write in the first letter of each word below.

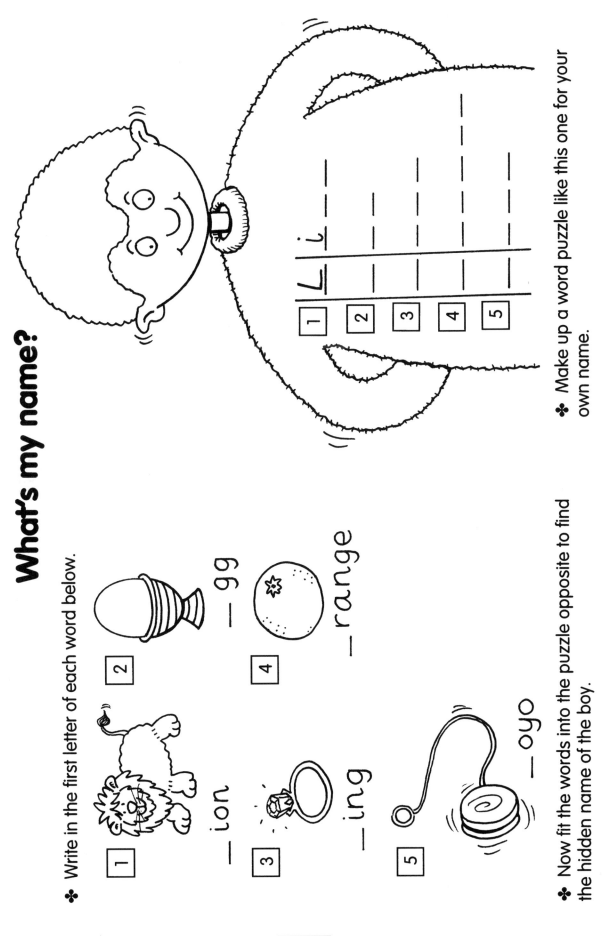

1	__ion
2	__gg
3	__ing
4	__range
5	__oyo

L i __ __ __ __ __

| 1 | 2 | 3 | 4 | 5 |

❖ Now fit the words into the puzzle opposite to find the hidden name of the boy.

♣ Make up a word puzzle like this one for your own name.

Find the vowels

Once upon a time there were three bears.

They lived in a cottage in the wood.

a b c d e f g h i j k l m n o p q r s t u v w x y z

a e i o and u are the **vowels**.

Words need vowels.

❖ Read the sentences in the flag.

❖ Colour the vowels yellow.

How many times did you colour 'e'?

❖ Colour the vowels on the three bears' cottage.

Name _____

Hide and seek

Jen is looking for her pets. They are hiding.

Can you help Jen find her pets?

✤ Fill in the letters to say where they are hiding.

p i g is in the h __ t

h __ n is in the b __ x

c __ t is in the b __ g

d __ g is in the b __ n

r __ t is in the p __ n

NO FUSS
PHOTOCOPIABLE

Name _____

Recognising rhyming words – 1

● Colour blue the words that rhyme with **bed**.

● Colour red the words that rhyme with **bat**.

● Colour green the words that rhyme with **pit**.

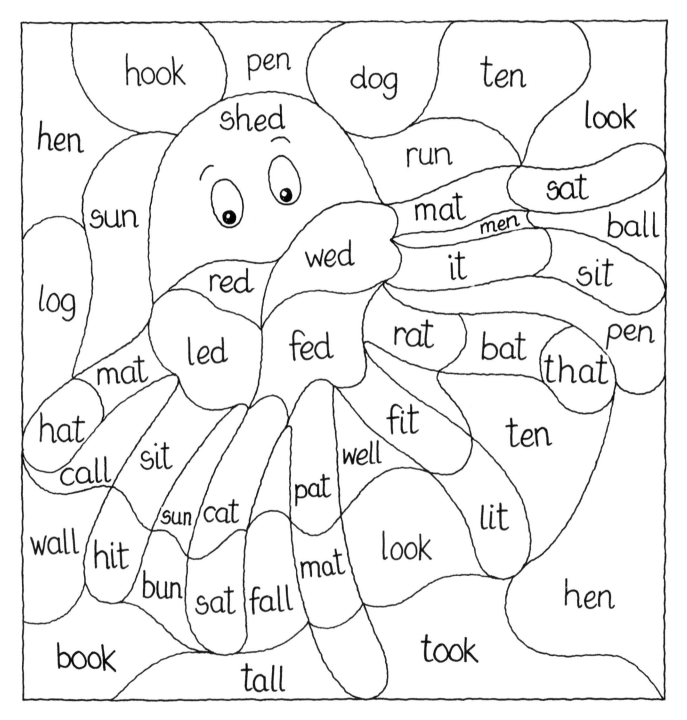

● What have you found? _____

Recognising rhyming words – 2

● Can you reach the gold by finding the rhyming path?

Start here

bold   man   frog   dog

went   old   hold   cold

had   cook   get   told

log   dog   fold   wall

ball   bold   hat   eat

sun   sold   gold

● Now use some of your rhyming words to put in these sentences.

Jack _____ the cow for five beans.

When they opened the sack it was full of _____ .

Chips or ships?

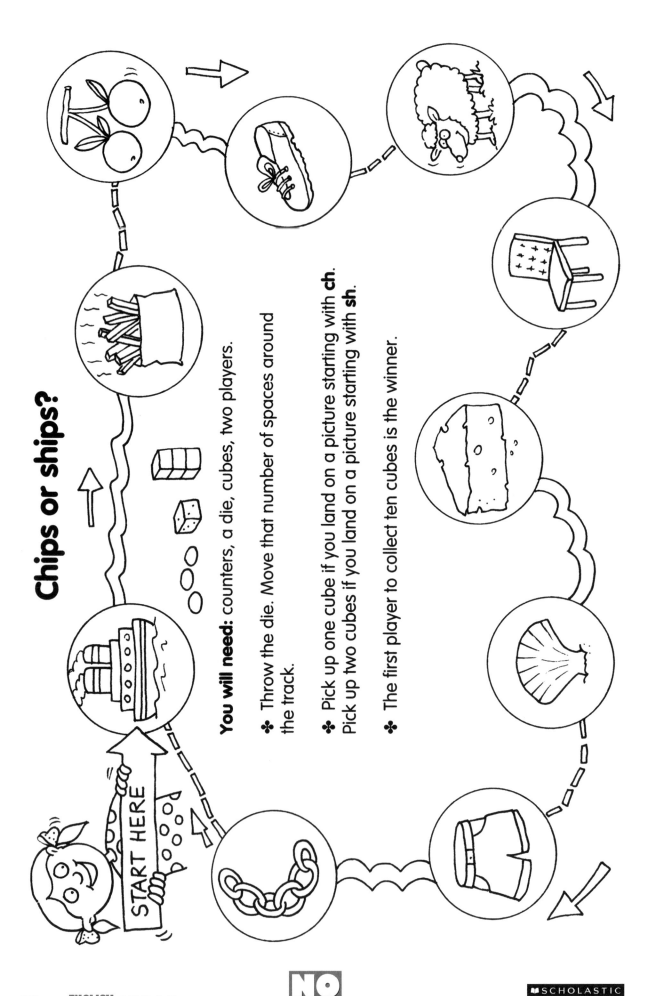

You will need: counters, a die, cubes, two players.

✤ Throw the die. Move that number of spaces around the track.

♣ Pick up one cube if you land on a picture starting with **ch**. Pick up two cubes if you land on a picture starting with **sh**.

♣ The first player to collect ten cubes is the winner.

START HERE

SCHOLASTIC
www.scholastic.co.uk

Thank you

Theo has written a **th**ank you letter.

✤ Read it and ring **th** at the beginning of words.

✤ Draw Theo opening his present in the space below. What did Aunt Thora send him?

✤ Show what **Th**eo is **th**inking in a **th**ought bubble.

Thursday 2nd May

Dear Aunt Thora,
Thank you for my present. I think it's great! It's nice and thick. You make lovely things.

Love from Theo x

What a noise!

The children have made a noisy band.

♣ Look at the picture. Use words starting with **wh** to finish the sentences.

Rica went **wham** on the ____ eelbarrow.

Dee went ____ izz on the ____ .

Don went ____ on the ____ .

Mrs White said ____ a noise!

wheel

whizz

whee

wham

wheelbarrow

whistle

Mrs **White**

Find the blends

● Can you find something in the picture that begins with the following letters? **pl, ch, cl, dr, tr, fl, sh, st, gl, sc**

● Write the letters on to the picture.

Today is Tuesday

Jason

LEROY

Lisa

Snail trail

❖ Fill in **ai** in the middle of the words.

❖ Draw the trail the snail made.

It went:
- over the cat's **tail**
- up the **chain**
- to the **nails**
- over the **train**
- in the **paint** pot.

❖ Can you draw some other trails the snail could make?

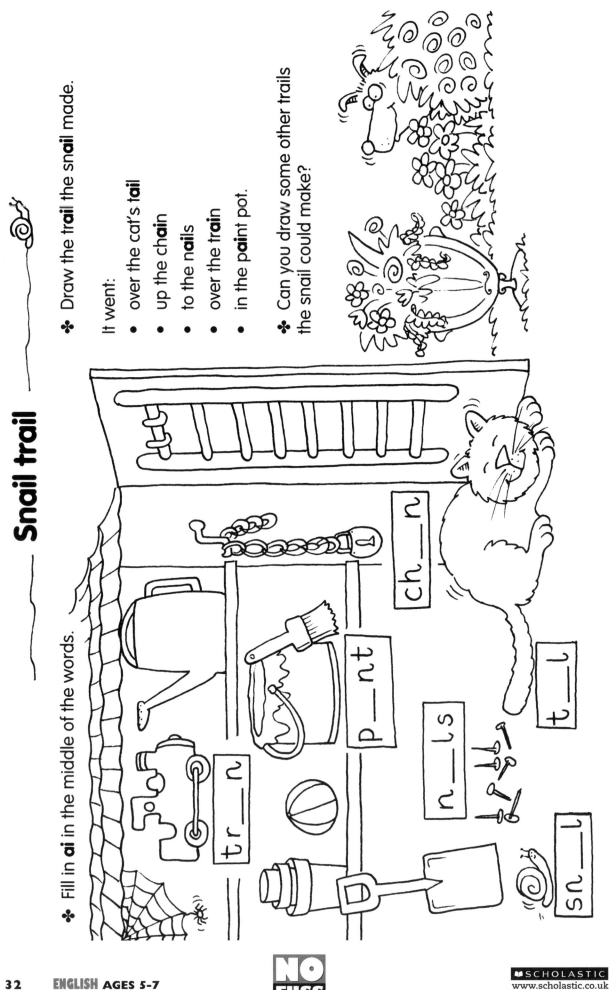

tr_n

p_nt

n_ls

ch_n

t_l

sn_l

Tell me...

♣ Fill in the missing **ea** in the middle of the words on these quiz cards.

♣ Cut out the cards.

♣ Place the cards face down in a pile. Take it in turns to turn them over and ask each other the questions on the card.

✂

Tell me one thing you never put on your h __ __ d.

Tell me what a robot has for br __ __ kfast.

Tell me two books you've r __ __ d.

Tell me about today's w __ __ ther.

Tell me two things you spr __ __ d.

Tell me two things you spr __ __ d on br __ __ d.

Tell me one thing that is h __ __ vier than a f __ __ ther.

Toad and Goat

sail on a **boat**

eat t**oa**st

He meets Goat. Goat has his cloak on.

Toad goes down the road in his new coat.

❧ Read the start of this story. Ring **oa** in the middle of the words.

❧ What do Toad and Goat do next? Below are some ideas.

ride on a **coach**

❧ Draw and write your ideas in the last box. Use some **oa** words.

NO FUSS
PHOTOCOPIABLE

Two of a kind?

✤ Which vowels double up in English words? Cut them out.

aa	ee	ii	oo	uu

✤ Now follow the example shown below and try out the consonants one after another at the **beginning** and **end** of the double vowels. See how many words you can make. Don't forget blends with **r** and **l**.

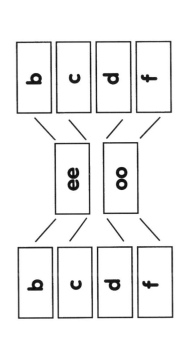

✤ Put your words to **good** use and finish this story:
'**D**eep in the w**oo**ds....'

✤ Cut out these consonants.

b	c	d
f	g	h
j	k	l
m	n	p
q	r	s
t	v	w
x	y	z

♣ Animal fun

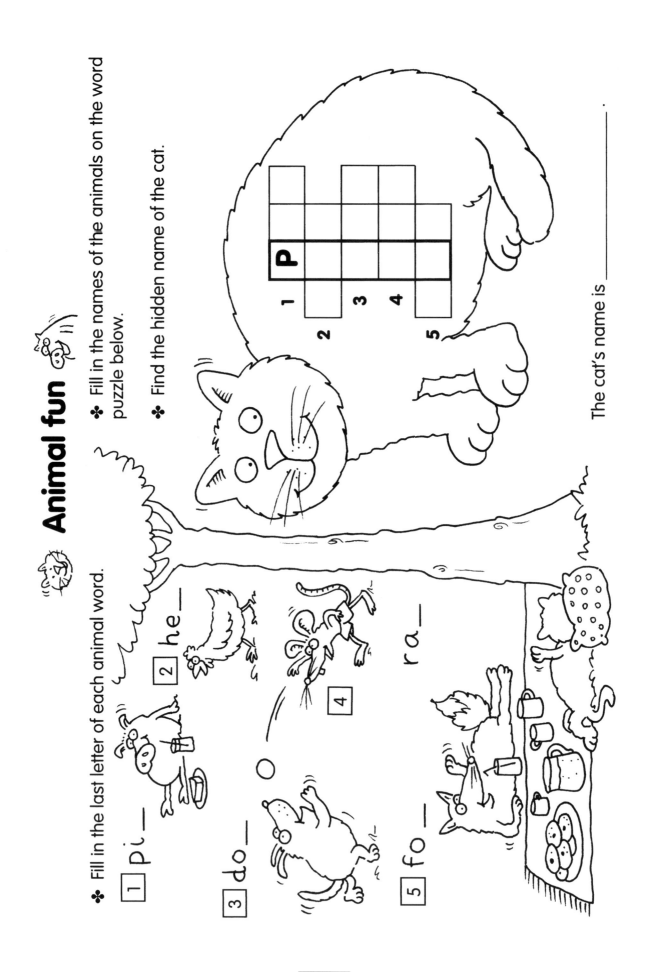

❖ Fill in the names of the animals on the word puzzle below.

❖ Find the hidden name of the cat.

❖ Fill in the last letter of each animal word.

1. pi_

2. he_

3. do_

4. [ra_]

5. fo_

The cat's name is _____

New clothes

Hippopotamus, Walrus and Octopus are trying on some new clothes.

♣ Fill in the missing **s** at the end of the words in the speech bubbles.

Pant_

tight_

Thi_ coat i_ very smart.

I'll need four pair_ of jean_.

Ye_. I like these short_.

♣ Tell the story of what is happening in the picture. Use lots of words ending with **s**.

Going into the past

✤ Can you add **-ed** on to the end of these verbs?

I look

I watch

I wait

I call

I answer

I listen

I learn

What have you done? You changed present actions into past ones.

✤ Can you change these present actions into past ones?

You hope

You joke

You dare

You imagine

You rejoice

You chase

You race

You escape

Did you realise that verbs ending in **-e** only have a **-d** added to change them into past actions?

✤ Now put these actions into the past. (**Watch out!** Verbs ending in **b, p** or **g** often double up these letters before adding -ed or -ing.)

They skip........, hop........, trip........, shop........,

tip........, rob........, beg........, hug........, tug........,

rub........, strip....... and stop........

My favourite -ing words

Do you like to...

sing,

chatter,

laugh,

drink,

eat,

go swimming

or shopping?

Perhaps you like to help or hurry or do you like to think, read, draw, dream, paint, play music, tricks or games?

What do you like to do?

❖ Fill this in, using as many -ing words as you can.

The things I like doing best are:

_____

_____

_____

and most of all, as you can see from my drawing here, I love

_____

In the playground: 1

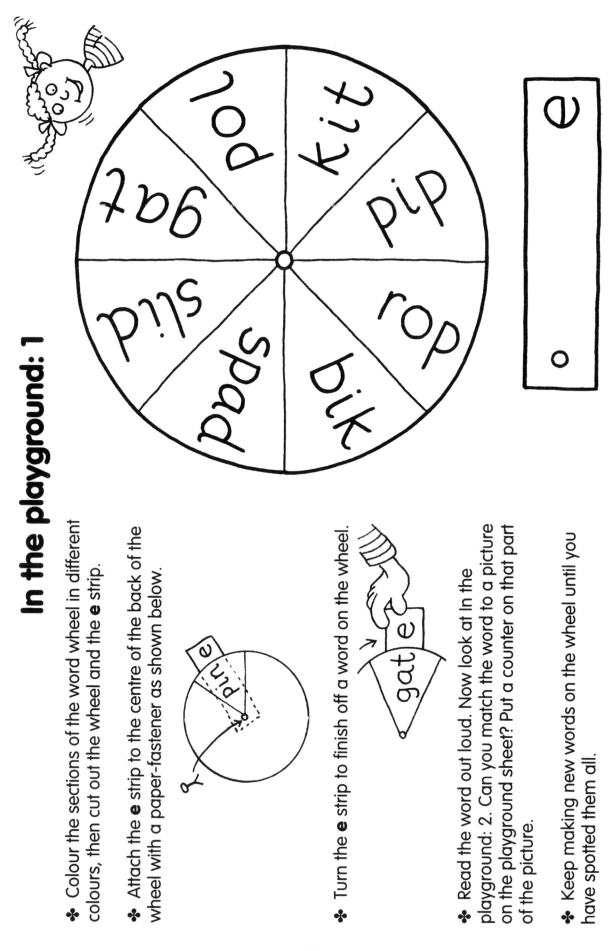

* Colour the sections of the word wheel in different colours, then cut out the wheel and the **e** strip.

* Attach the **e** strip to the centre of the back of the wheel with a paper-fastener as shown below.

* Turn the **e** strip to finish off a word on the wheel.

* Read the word out loud. Now look at In the playground: 2. Can you match the word to a picture on the playground sheet? Put a counter on that part of the picture.

* Keep making new words on the wheel until you have spotted them all.

NO FUSS PHOTOCOPIABLE

www.scholastic.co.uk

Name _____

In the playground: 2

Use this sheet with In the playground: 1.

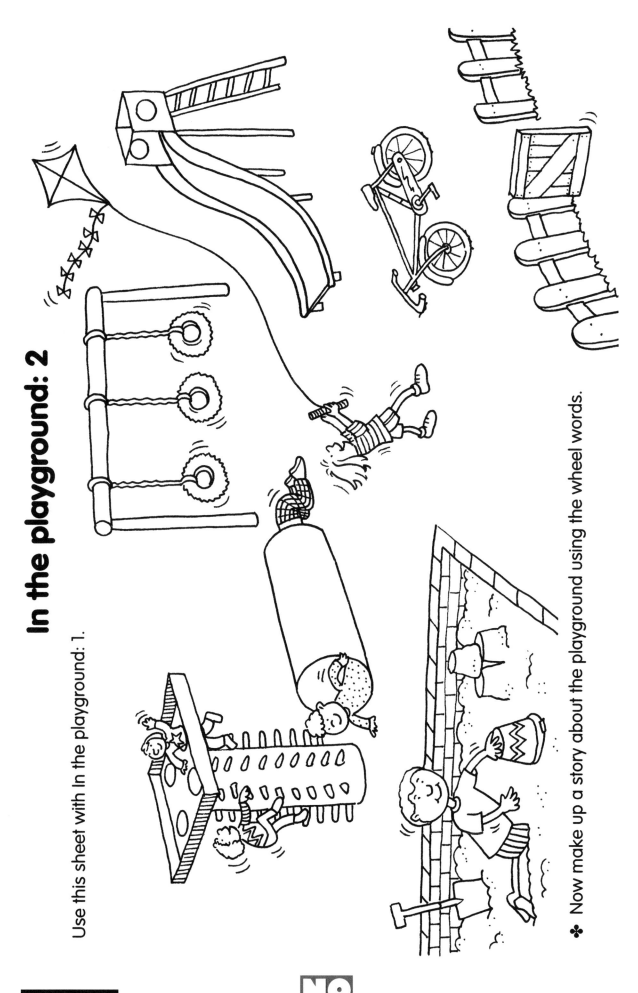

✿ Now make up a story about the playground using the wheel words.

Spell it to music

♣ Make up as many words as you can from the musical notes A to G. You can use each letter more than once. It might help if you organise them alphabetically.

A	B	C	D
ace	bad bag		

E	F	G

♣ Now your friends can play your words on chime bars.

• Write the words clearly on a large sheet of paper.

• Conduct your orchestra through the list of words, pointing at each letter.

• Sing the letters together as the musicians strike the right chime bar.

• Keep a steady beat at first. You can speed up to make it more difficult, if you like.

G F E D C B A

SCHOLASTIC
www.scholastic.co.uk

A jumbo muddle

elephant

❖ In the space below make as many words as you can out of the word elephant.

You can use each letter in elephant once in each word.

❖ What is the difference between an African and an Indian elephant?

Picture sums

Sometimes two words can be put together to make a new word. For example:

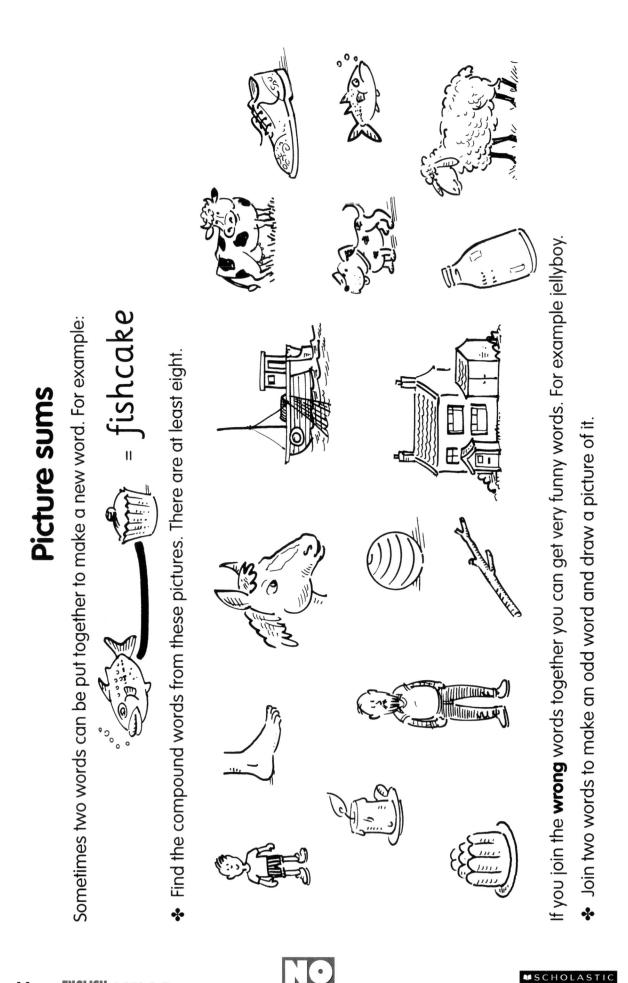

= fishcake

✤ Find the compound words from these pictures. There are at least eight.

If you join the **wrong** words together you can get very funny words. For example jellyboy.

✤ Join two words to make an odd word and draw a picture of it.

Name _____

Take your partner

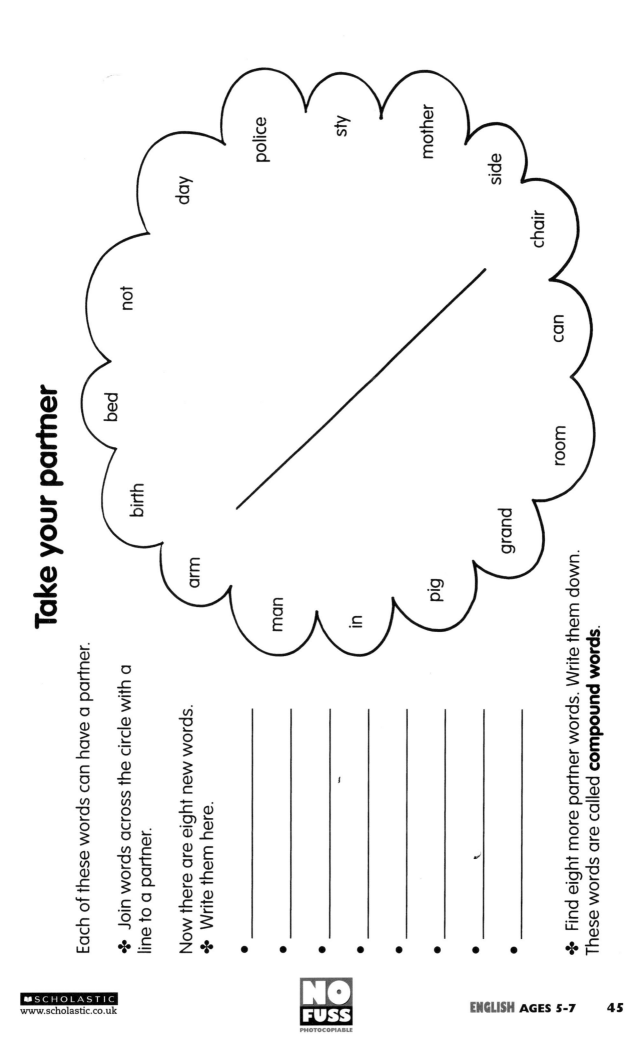

Each of these words can have a partner.

❖ Join words across the circle with a line to a partner.

Now there are eight new words.
❖ Write them here.

• _____
• _____
• _____
• _____
• _____
• _____
• _____
• _____

❖ Find eight more partner words. Write them down. These words are called **compound words**.

Homophones

Homophones are words that **sound** the **same** but are spelled differently
and have a different meaning.
❖ Link the pairs of homophones with a line.

❖ Take it in turns to describe one of the pairs and give a clue to the first letter.
For example, 'I'm thinking of a pair of homophones beginning with 'd', one is
an animal and one you use when writing a letter'. [**Answer**: deer and dear].
• Score one point for guessing correctly.
• Score two more points for spelling **both** words correctly.

Name _____

Sounds like...

Here are some words that sound alike.

♣ Draw the right picture for each thing and cross out the wrong word.

a fruit	an animal		to lock things with
pear pair	hair hare		quay key
a plant	animal feet	a bucket	an animal
flower flour	pause paws	beach beech	a bucket
		pail pale	bare bear

Do you know the meaning of all the words crossed out?

♣ Check them in a dictionary if you're not sure.

Opposite sides – opposite words

♣ Cut out and fold these cards. Then fill in the opposite word on the back of each one.

♣ Ask a friend to guess the hidden opposite word.

✂

on off	down	cold	slow
out	friend	back
under	dark	heavy	left	noisy

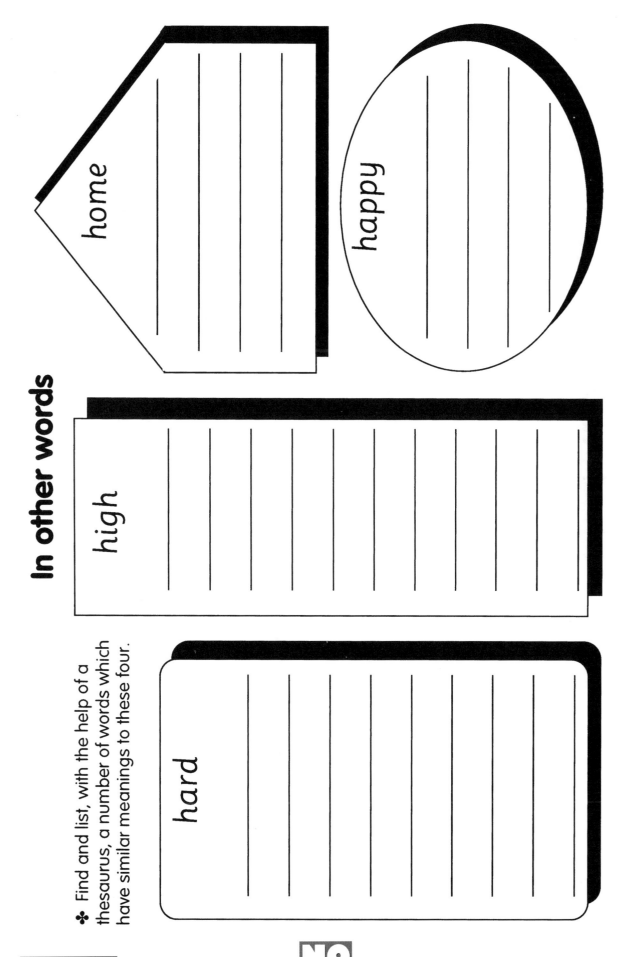

home

happy

In other words

high

hard

✤ Find and list, with the help of a thesaurus, a number of words which have similar meanings to these four.

Mehndi patterns

In some countries people decorate their hands for special occasions.
❖ Use the patterns shown to decorate your hand.

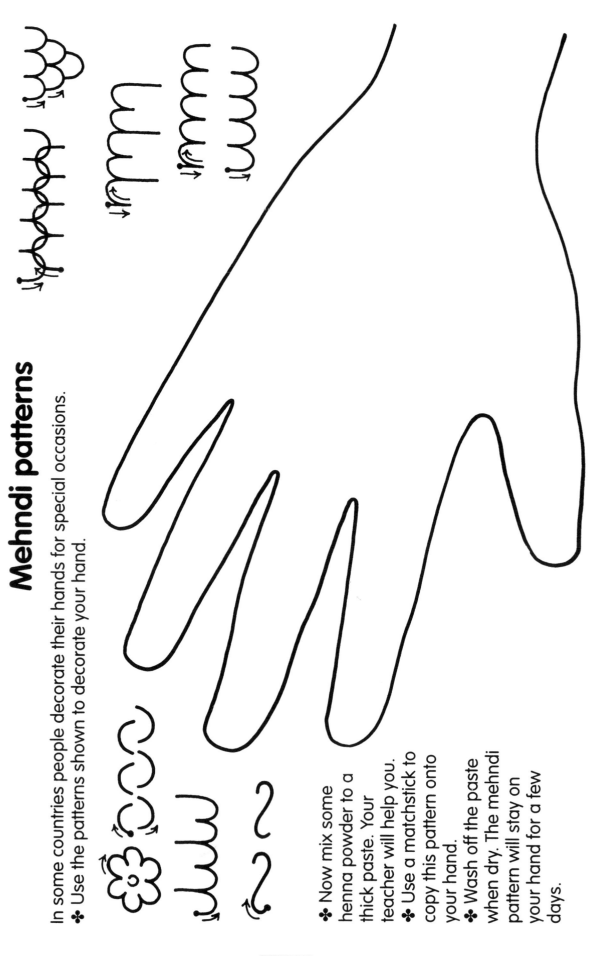

❖ Now mix some henna powder to a thick paste. Your teacher will help you.
❖ Use a matchstick to copy this pattern onto your hand.
❖ Wash off the paste when dry. The mehndi pattern will stay on your hand for a few days.

SCHOLASTIC
www.scholastic.co.uk

Name _____

Knitting with Mrs Mopple

✤ Help Mrs Mopple with her knitting.

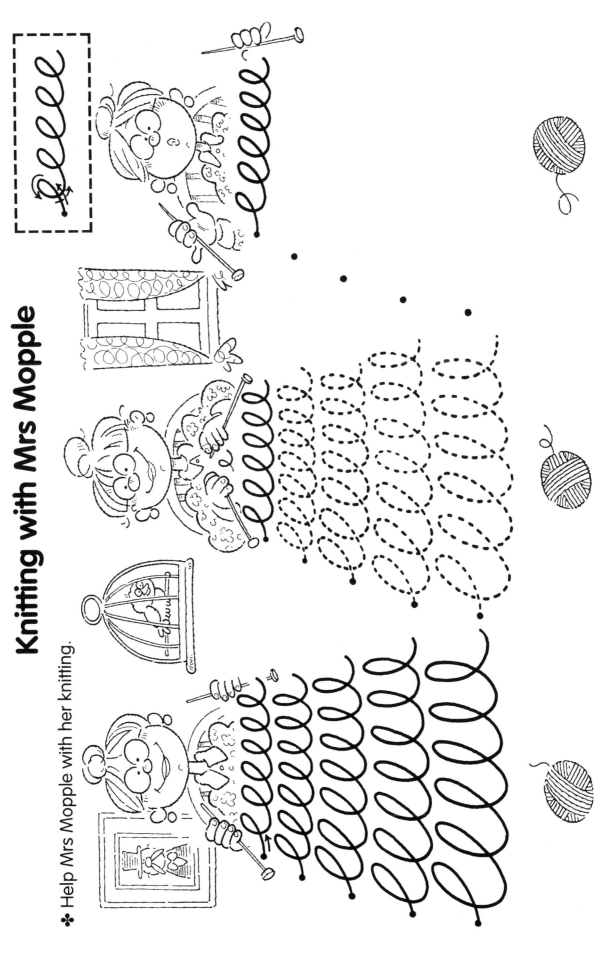

Aliens

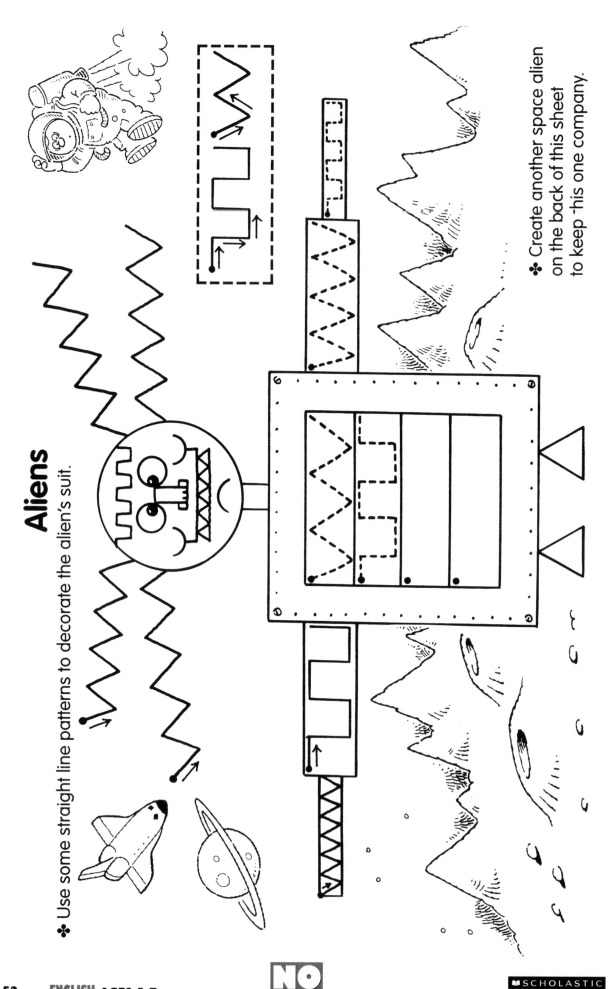

❖ Use some straight line patterns to decorate the alien's suit.

❖ Create another space alien on the back of this sheet to keep this one company.

SCHOLASTIC
www.scholastic.co.uk

Umbrella pattern

● Finish the picture and the border. Make the lines and patterns go the same way. Don't use a ruler.

Feed the caterpillar

Caterpillars love eating.
❖ Fill in the caterpillar's tummy with alphabet spaghetti!

yum yum!

❖ Don't forget the legs!
❖❖ Find out what caterpillars really like to eat.

NO FUSS PHOTOCOPIABLE

SCHOLASTIC
www.scholastic.co.uk

Beautiful butterfly

❖ Decorate this butterfly using these letters:

❖ Where do butterflies come from?

❖ Remember to make the two wings the same!

Quilt covers

♣ Use the letters **v**, **w**, **x** and **z** to design quilt covers for Snow White and the dwarfs.

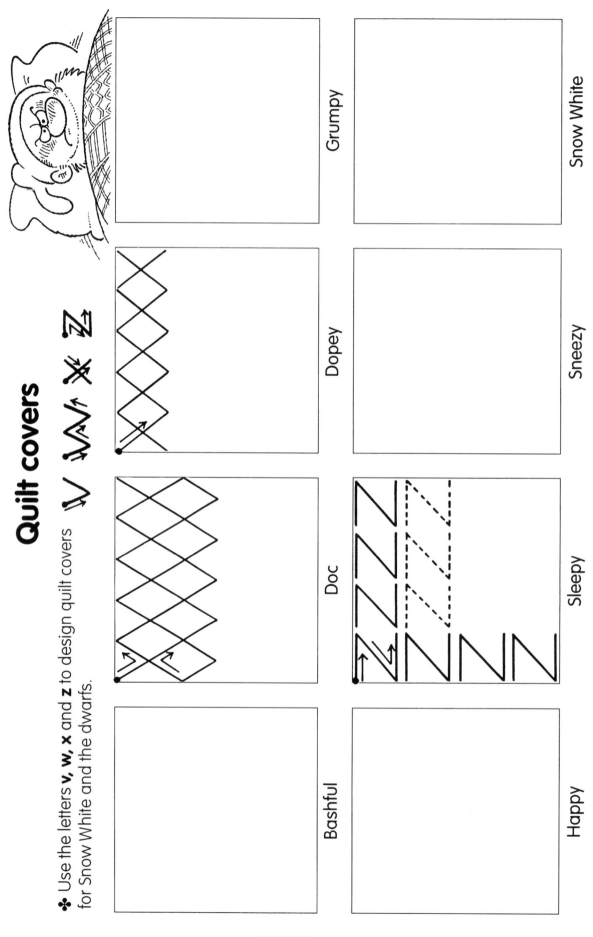

Grumpy

Snow White

Dopey

Sneezy

Doc

Sleepy

Bashful

Happy

SCHOLASTIC
www.scholastic.co.uk

Party time

♣ Design a sheet of wrapping paper using three of the letters in this family:

c o a d g q e

♣ Write about your favourite birthday present ever.

Name _____

Peacock feathers

❖ Practise the letter **f**.

❖ Use lots of **f**'s to decorate the peacock's tail.

SCHOLASTIC
www.scholastic.co.uk

Name _____

Special k / k

You can write the letter **k** like this: ↓↘k²

❖ Draw over the letters below.

k k k k k

❖ Make a porcupine using this letter **k**.

Remember
Keep turning the paper round to do his whole body.

You can also write **k** like this: ↓k²

❖ Draw over the letters below.

k k k k k k

❖ Make two hedgehogs using this letter **k**.

❖ Which one do you find easier to write: **k** or **k**?

Hisssss!

Sometimes we write the letter **s** like this: ᔓ

✤ Practise this **s** then decorate the snake skins.

S S S S S S S S S S S

Sometimes we write the letter **s** like this: ᕁ

✤ Practise this ᕁ then decorate the snake skins.

ᕁ ᕁ ᕁ ᕁ ᕁ ᕁ ᕁ ᕁ ᕁ ᕁ ᕁ

This ᕁ joins up more easily with other letters.

✤ Find out why a snake sheds its skin.

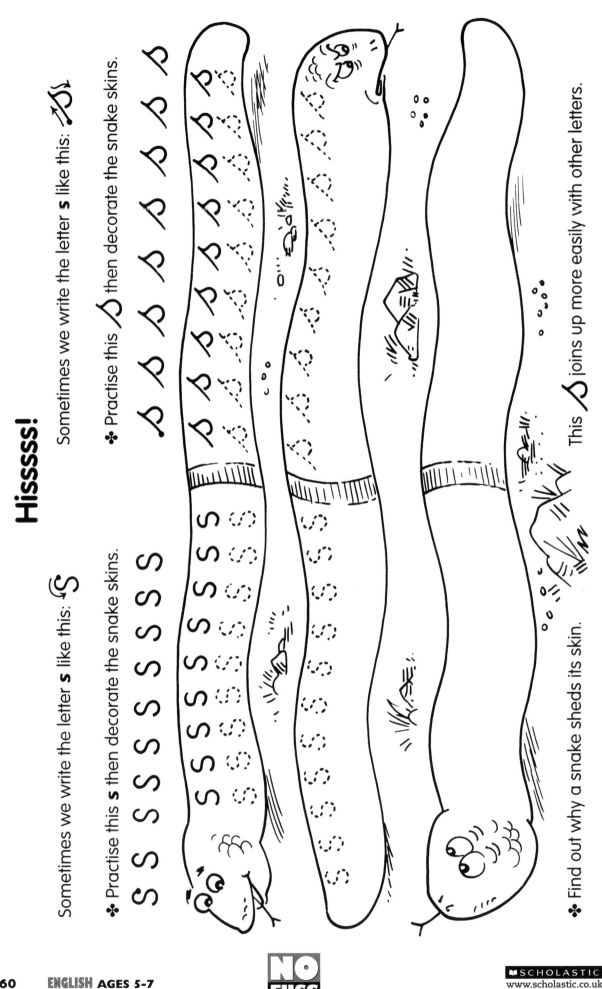

■ SCHOLASTIC
www.scholastic.co.uk

Sign here!

Important notices are often written in capital letters.

❖ Write these signs out in full.

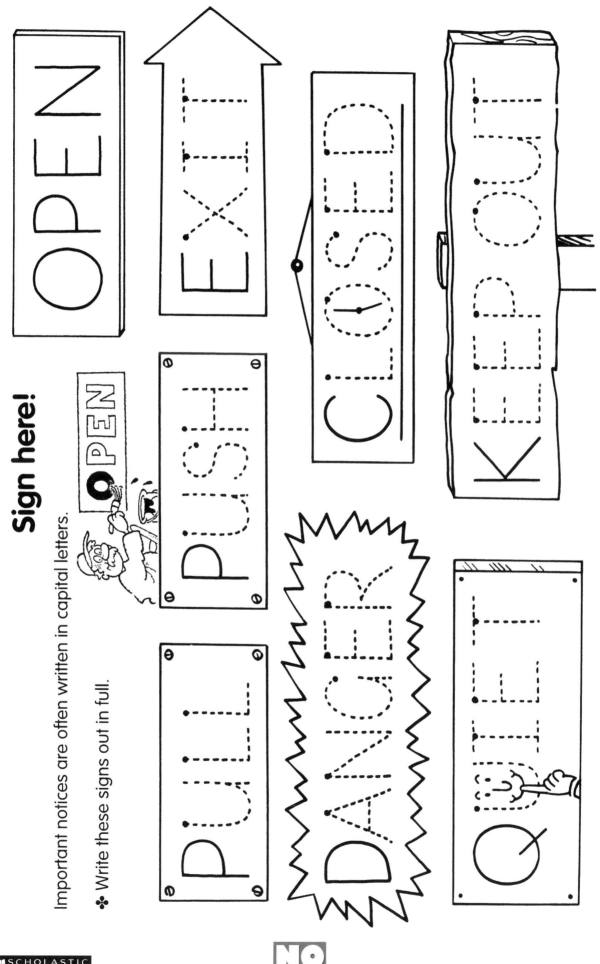

OPEN EXIT CLOSED KEEP OUT

OPEN PUSH DANGER QUIET

PULL

Placemats

❖ Decorate these placemats with words you write every day.

me me me

it it it

in in in

by by by

my my my

he he he

❖ Now turn over this sheet and try writing them with your eyes closed.

NO FUSS
PHOTOCOPIABLE

■SCHOLASTIC
www.scholastic.co.uk

Curtains

Take care! These letters join from the top: oven win visit old who

✤ Practise the letters below to finish decorating these curtains.

ob oe oh oi

ok ol om on

oo op or ot

ou ov ow

ve vi vo

vu vy

we wi wo

wh wn wt

Build a sentence – journeys

● Join the two parts of each sentence. Then write the sentences on the lines below.

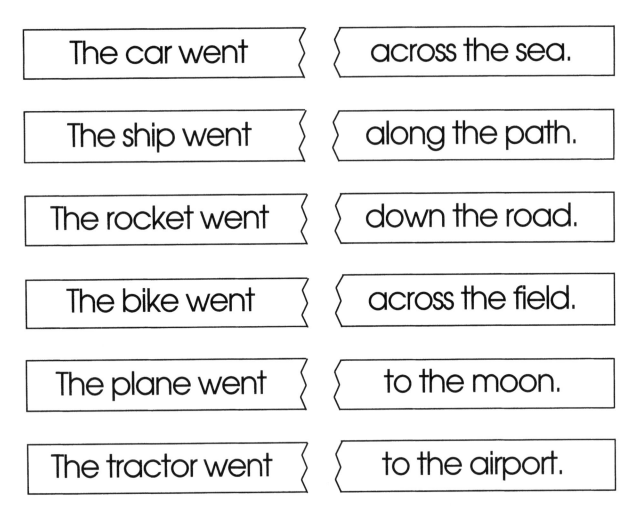

The car went	across the sea.
The ship went	along the path.
The rocket went	down the road.
The bike went	across the field.
The plane went	to the moon.
The tractor went	to the airport.

_____

_____

_____

_____

_____

Name _____

A train journey

✤ Cut and fold these engines and carriages.

✤ See how many different sentences you can make from them.

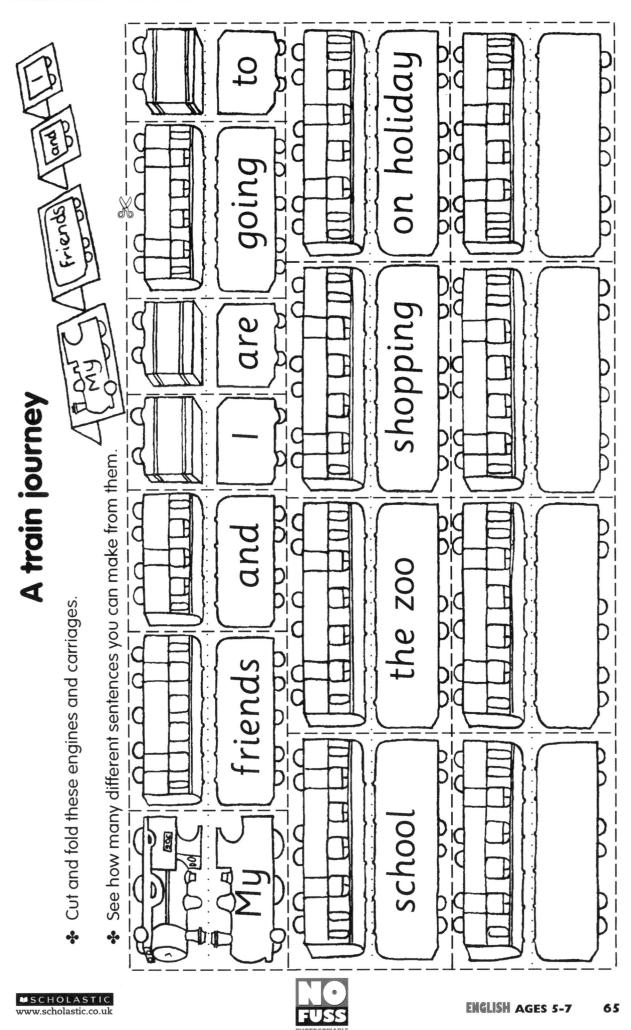

Off we go on the train

✤ Fill in the words to finish the sentences.

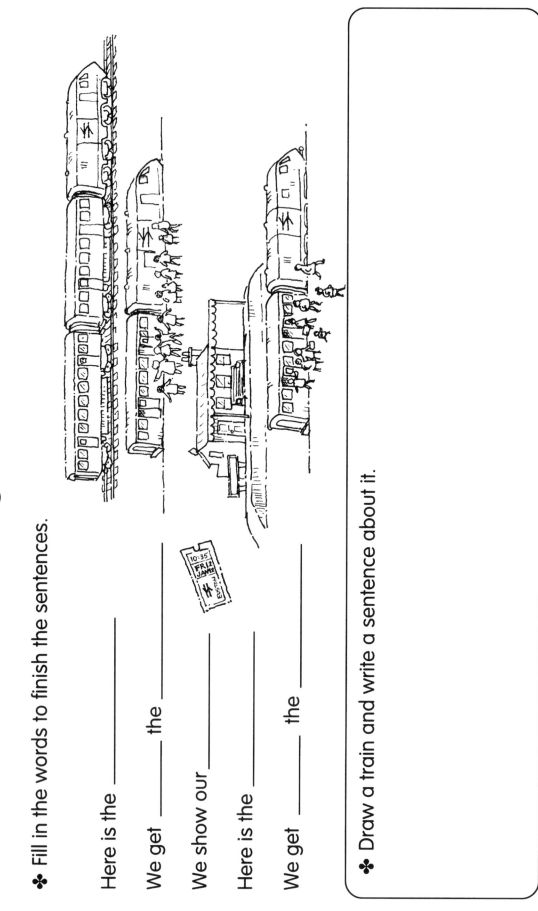

Here is the _____

We get _____ the _____

We show our _____

Here is the _____

We get _____ the _____

✤ Draw a train and write a sentence about it.

Name _____

Missing words

✿ Put the words in the right spaces.

to	had	you

there	to	the

Cinderella	sister	shoes

Once upon a time _____ was a girl named _____ the ball,

_____. She wanted to go _____ the ball,

but she _____ no dress and no _____.

'I want to go _____ the ball,' said Cinderella.

'_____ can't go,' said her _____.

'You have to clean _____ house.'

✿ Draw some pictures to show what happens in the story.

All mixed up

The words in these sentences are all mixed up.

✤ Write the sentences out again with the words in the
right order. Then read the funny story that they tell.

Smith is Mr greengrocer. a

_____

six is He tall. feet

_____

has hair. He brown

_____

coat. wears green He a

_____

does weigh? he What

_____

weighs He potatoes.

_____

■S C H O L A S T I C
www.scholastic.co.uk

Name _____

Name the object!

A **noun** is a word used as the name of a person, place or thing.

✤ Fill in the labels with the nouns which 'name' the pictures below.

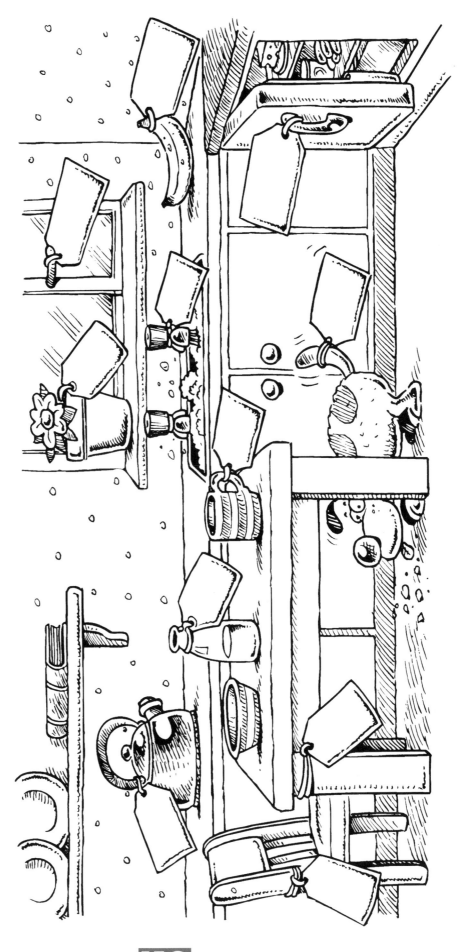

phone	car	book	radio
school	house	computer	pool
cake	dog	hat	library
bag	bridge	lamp	jelly
camera	tree	key	dream

✂

Word inventions

✤ Cut up the nouns.

✤ Put them together in different pairs, such as:

car	phone		library	book

✤ Think about what a **cake tree** or a **dog hat** might look like.

✤ Try drawing some of the new objects you have invented. Use the back of this sheet if you wish.

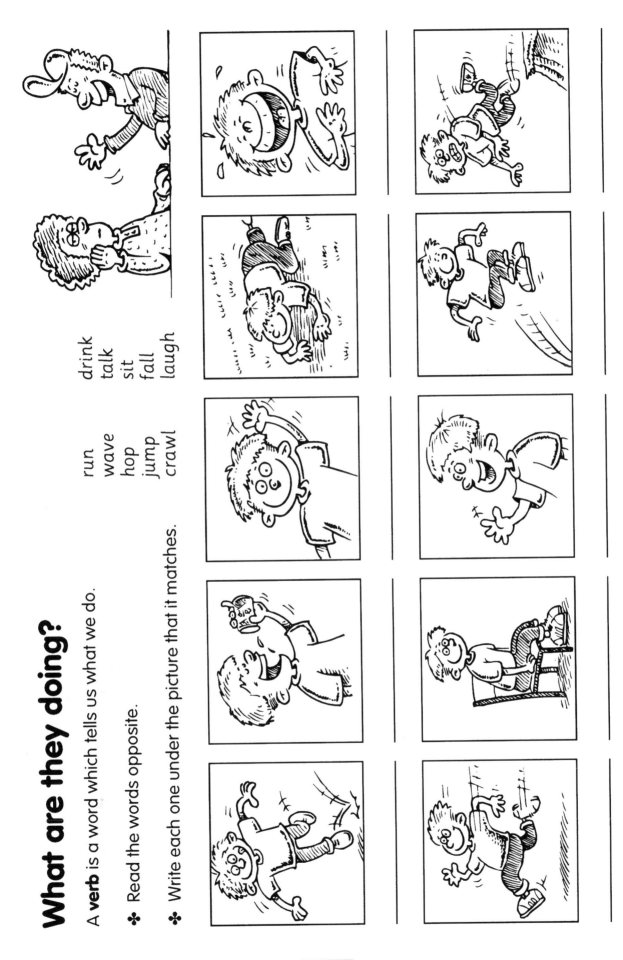

What are they doing?

A **verb** is a word which tells us what we do.

✿ Read the words opposite.

✿ Write each one under the picture that it matches.

drink
talk
sit
fall
laugh

run
wave
hop
jump
crawl

Name _____

Name _____

In the future

We use the **future tense** of verbs to talk about what we are going to do or what will happen in the future.

♣ Read the speech bubbles. Underline the future tense verbs. The first one has been done for you.

♣ Write about what you would like to do in the future.

Speech bubbles:
- I will make people laugh.
- I am going to drive a high speed train.
- I will go to the cinema next week.
- I am going to be an astronaut.
- Do you think we'll travel to Mars?
- I shall be working in a library.
- You shall go to the ball Cinderella.
- I will explore the rainforest.

SCHOLASTIC
www.scholastic.co.uk

What did you do?

We use the **past tense** to tell about what we have done.

♣ Write a story about something you did a long time ago.

In my day, we didn't have computers to play with. We played with marbles and listened to the wireless.

♣ Look back at the verbs you used. Underline the ones that are in the past tense.

Who did what?

A **pronoun** is a word which replaces a noun, such as:

| they | him | her | us | he | she | them | it |

✤ Look at the pronouns above.

✤ Use them to replace the underlined words.

The robber stole jewels and hid the jewels under his bed.

The next day the robber looked for the jewels.

'The jewels have gone!' the robber cried.

'Do you mean that bag of junk?' said his mother.

'I gave the bag to the police jumble sale.'

'Oh no!' said the robber.

So his mother told the robber she was sorry.

SCHOLASTIC
www.scholastic.co.uk

He, she, it

❖ Read the story below.

❖ Replace all the underlined nouns with pronouns.

Rosy went to town. Sam bought <u>Rosy</u> _____ a cake. Rosy gave

<u>the cake</u> _____ to Dan. <u>Dan</u> _____ invited Rosy and Sam

to tea. <u>Dan and Rosy and Sam</u> _____ ate the cake together.

Pronouns:

they	me	I

you	her	she

him	it

❖ Read this nonsense rhyme.

❖ Circle the pronouns.

They told me you had been to her,

And mentioned me to him:

She gave me a good character,

But said I could not swim.

Lewis Carroll

A dragon in the playground

● Use the pictures and words in the boxes to help you write your story.

Nouns		Verbs		Adjectives	
fire	teachers	scared	feed	friendly	gentle
scales	teeth	breathing	rode	lonely	hungry
smoke	nostrils	running	moving	surprised	heavy
school	tail	laughed	patted	enormous	angry

Name it

✤ Look at the names below. Write them on the register. Put in the capital letters. Add your own name, and mark where it would go.

- joshua carr
- andrew bennett
- karen mills
- jane williams
- carl rogers
- mandy newton

Register

dr _ _ _ _ nn _ _ _ t

_ _ _ h _ a _ _ rr

r _ n _ _ _ ls

_ _ _ _ d _ _ t _ n

r _ _ _ g _ r _

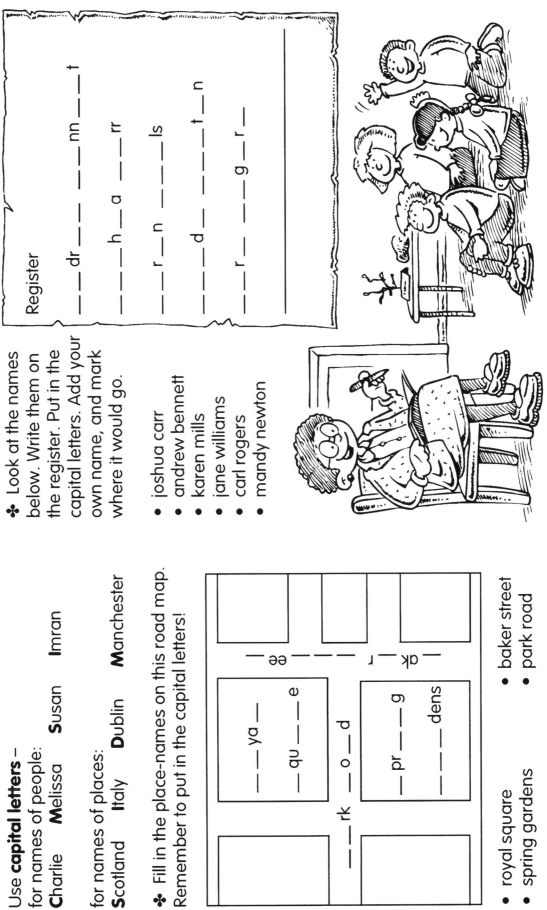

Use **capital letters** – for names of people:
Charlie **M**elissa **S**usan Imran

for names of places:
Scotland Italy **D**ublin **M**anchester

♣ Fill in the place-names on this road map. Remember to put in the capital letters!

_ _ _ ya _

qu _ _ e

_ e e

rk _ o _ d

pr _ _ g _ dens

_ _ _ k _ r

- royal square
- spring gardens
- baker street
- park road

Riddle muddle

A riddle is a kind of question.
Some riddles, and their answers, are
given below, but they are all mixed up!

❧ Cut out the cards.
❧ Put a question mark at the end of each riddle.
❧ Then match the answers to the riddles.

✂ - - - - - - - - - - - - - - - - - - -

A mushroom	How can you make varnish disappear
Where does afternoon come before morning	A shoe
Take the 'r' out of it.	How many sides does a house have
What always travels on foot	In the dictionary
What room has no walls and no door	Two – the inside and the outside

❖ Find or make up some more riddles of your own.

❖ Write them on a separate sheet of paper.

❖ Ask a friend to solve them.

Name _____

Guess the questions

Adam and Sara went to interview Zelma Bizarre the famous fortune teller. Zelma can see into the future, so she gave the answers before they asked the questions!

✤ Write the questions that Adam and Sara wanted to ask. Don't forget the question marks!

1	In a small town by the sea.
2	I always wash them on Thursdays.
3	I found them under a rock in the desert.
4	Fifty times around the garden every morning.
5	Six cats and four hamsters.
6	I've never done that in my life.

Take a break!

Commas are used to show when to pause.

In my pencil-case there are six pencils, an ink pen, some crayons, a pencil-sharpener, two erasers, three paper-clips, an old crisp and a note from my friend.

✤ Add the commas to this list.

In my bag I have six books three folders four stale crusts seven chocolate bar wrappers a plastic frog six football stickers and lots of scrap paper.

✤ Write a list of the things in your pencil-case, bag or pocket. If you can't find anything interesting you can make it up!

Watching television – what are they saying?

● Look at the picture. What is everyone saying? Write their words in the speech bubbles.

Name _____

What are they saying?

❖ Put the words in the right order then write the sentences into the bubbles.

me together Put again. back	any you Have wool?
what Grandma eyes Oh you big have!	frog. kiss want I don't to a
axe! get Quick an me	me house. Take Cinderella's to

Name _____

Make a new rhyme

● Write the words in the spaces.

ten

eyes

toes

I have _____ long fingers
And I have ten tiny _____
I have two bright _____
But I've only one _____

nose

● Write the words in the spaces.

mat

I have a pretty little _____
She likes to sit upon a _____
And when I stroke her silky _____
My pretty little _____ will purr.

fur

cat

Name _____

My lunch box

Colour the pictures. Cut them out and make a story.

SCHOLASTIC
www.scholastic.co.uk

Completing stories – the big puddle

● Sort out the sentences to find out who said what.

'Oh, you naughty boy!'   *'This is fun,'*   *'I went in one little puddle,'*

'Did you go in any puddles?'   *'I will jump in it,'*

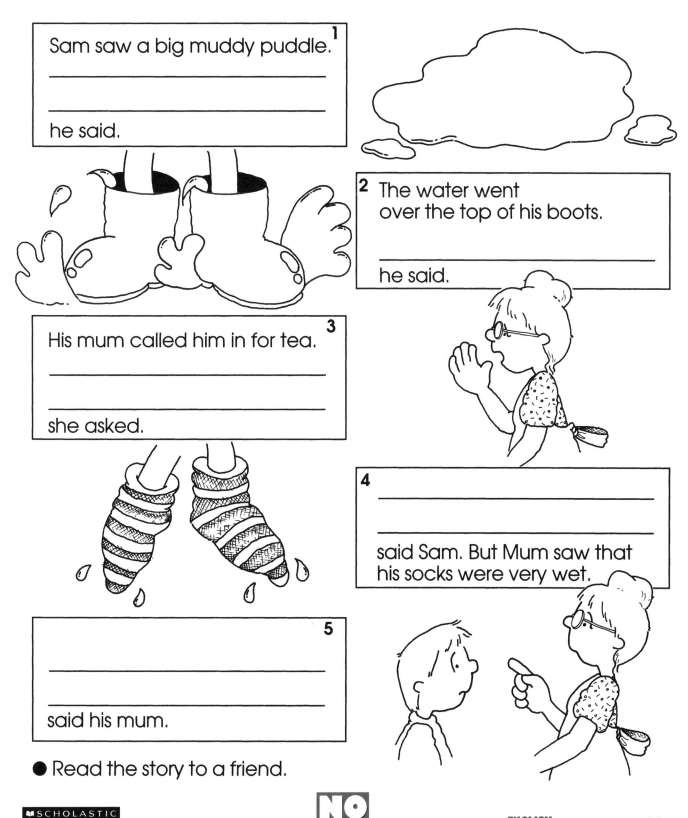

Sam saw a big muddy puddle. ¹
_____
_____
he said.

2 The water went
over the top of his boots.
_____
he said.

His mum called him in for tea. ³
_____
_____
she asked.

4 _____
_____
said Sam. But Mum saw that
his socks were very wet.

5 _____
_____
said his mum.

● Read the story to a friend.

The wind and the sun

Colour the pictures. Cut out the paragraphs.
Put them in order to tell the story.

'Now it is my turn,' said the sun
and he began to shine.
It got hotter and hotter.

The wind saw that the sun had tricked him.
He was so cross that he howled and
blew over the mountains.

1

The wind thought he was stronger than the sun.
'Very well,' said the sun.
'Let us see who is the stronger.'

'I shall be first,' said the wind and
he began to blow.
But the harder he blew the more
the man wrapped his jacket around him.

The sun saw a man walking down the road.
'The one who can make the man
take off his jacket is the stronger,' said the sun.

'This is a very hot day,' said the man
and he took off his jacket.

NO FUSS
PHOTOCOPIABLE

Picture story writing – the caves

● Draw the missing pictures and write the missing text. Now finish the story.

1	**2**
One sunny day the children wanted to have a picnic. Mum said, 'You can go to the beach but do not go in the caves.'	_____ _____ _____ _____
3	**4**
The cave was dark and damp and not interesting at all. They turned to leave when they saw water lapping around their feet. The tide was coming in!	_____ _____ _____ _____

Language map

❖ Look at this 'language map' of a school dinner hall.

❖ Try to listen to the things people say – at home, in school, in the street, at the swimming baths...

❖ Make your own 'language map' of a place you know well in the box below. Give it a title.

I don't like custard on beans!

Stay in the line!

Don't sit on the packed lunch table!

I've got yoghurt on my nose.

Can I go out now? please?

Put your trays here.

Sit down Charlotte!

■ SCHOLASTIC
www.scholastic.co.uk

What would you like?

❖ Choose two things for Max and two things for Mary.

What will Max and Mary say to the waitress?

Words to help you

	toast	please
I	beans	
like		burger	chips
would		
fruit juice	hot dog	milk shake

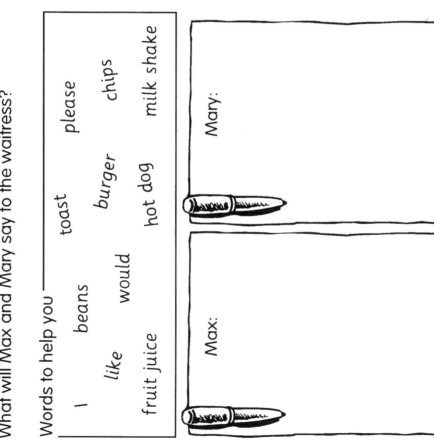

Mary:

Max:

Different story types

Story types

horror

fairy

adventure

sport

animal

crime

❖ Match up each picture with the right story type.

❖ List as many other story types as you can on the back of this sheet.

SWAG

NO FUSS
PHOTOCOPIABLE

SCHOLASTIC
www.scholastic.co.uk

Choose-your-own fairy story

● Choose the pictures to make the story.

Once upon a time there was a

who lived in a

One day, a

came along who

and the

turned into a

● Now read <u>your</u> story to a friend.

Identikit pictures

● Read the descriptions, then draw the characters.

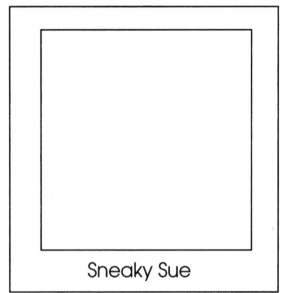

Sneaky Sue

She has long hair.
She wears glasses.
Her ears stick out.
She has crooked teeth.

Robber Joe

He wears a black patch.
He has a scar below his lip.
He has no front teeth.
His hair is black.

● Look at the pictures, then choose their names and write their descriptions.

_____   _____

_____   _____

How do they feel?

How does the girl feel? Why?

How does the driver feel? Why?

How do the children feel? Why?

How does the farmer feel? Why?

MY MONSTER

✤ You are going to make up a monster.
Fill in the spaces and tick the boxes which best describe it.

All about my monster

Drawing of monster

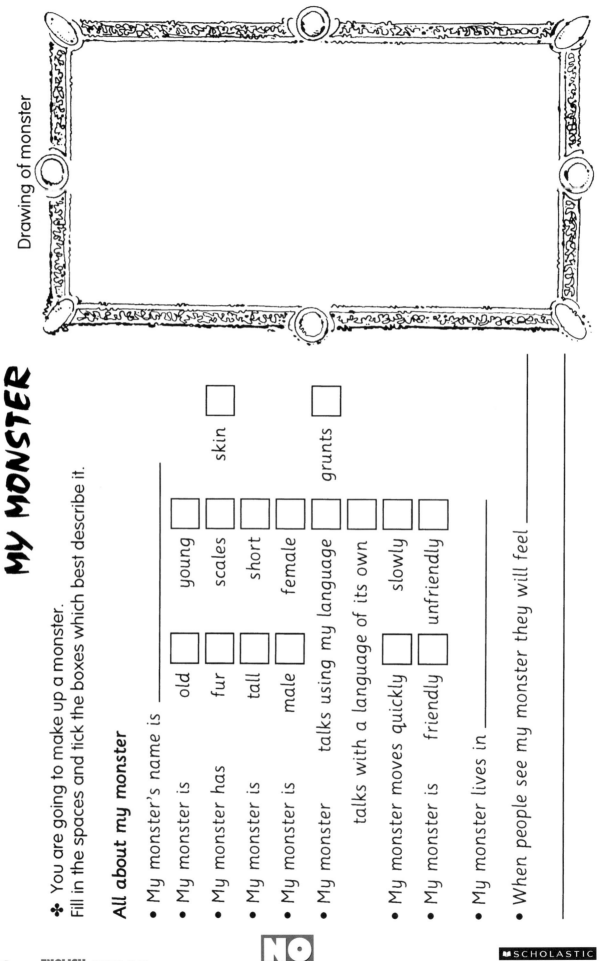

● My monster's name is _____

● My monster is ☐ old ☐ young

● My monster has ☐ fur ☐ scales ☐ skin

● My monster is ☐ tall ☐ short

● My monster is ☐ male ☐ female

● My monster ☐ talks using my language ☐ grunts
☐ talks with a language of its own

● My monster moves ☐ quickly ☐ slowly

● My monster is ☐ friendly ☐ unfriendly

● My monster lives in _____

● When people see my monster they will feel _____

SCHOLASTIC
www.scholastic.co.uk

MY MONSTER STORY

Choose one of the following monster story openings and continue the story.

- Icy mist swirled around the entrance to the cave.

- Amanda sat up in bed feeling terrified. She was sure she could hear scurrying sounds outside.

- Thud! Thud!
Two huge feet moved slowly through the long, wet grass.

To think about

Where will your story be set?

Will the monster try to talk to people?

What will children think of the monster?

What will the monster eat?

Will the end of the story be happy or sad?

A story train

✤ Cut and fold to make the engines and carriages.

✤ How many different story openings can you make?

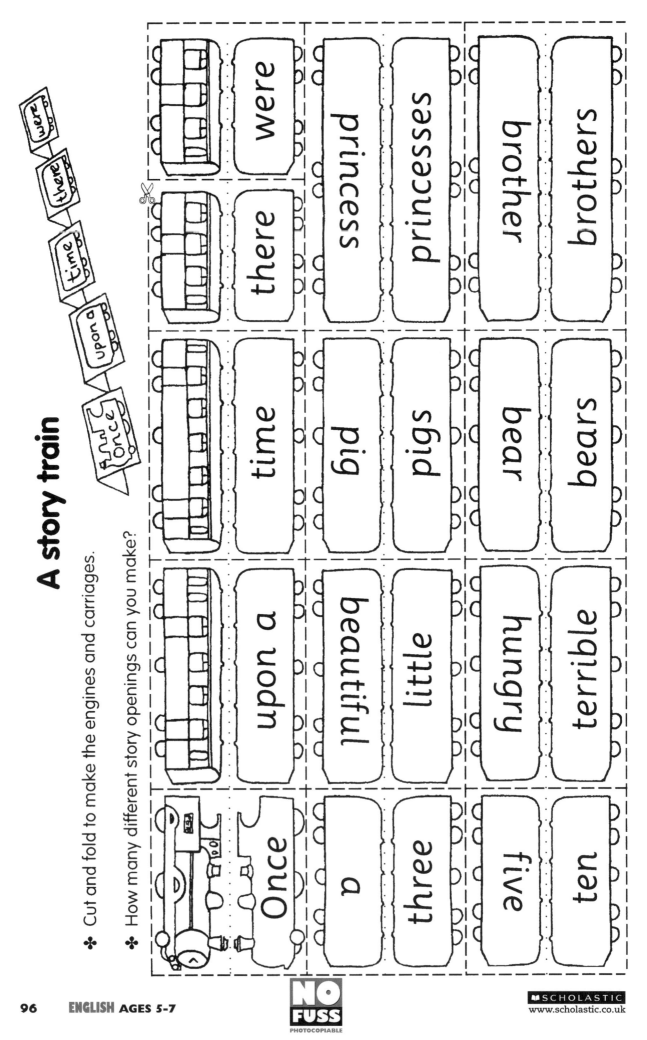

■SCHOLASTIC
www.scholastic.co.uk

Writing story openings

♣ Write a story opening for each of these pictures.
Try to write the opening using the way to start which is written beside each picture.

Describe the place.

Describe the character.

Write what the characters are saying.

Describe what is happening.

Chain of events

❖ Complete this chain of events.

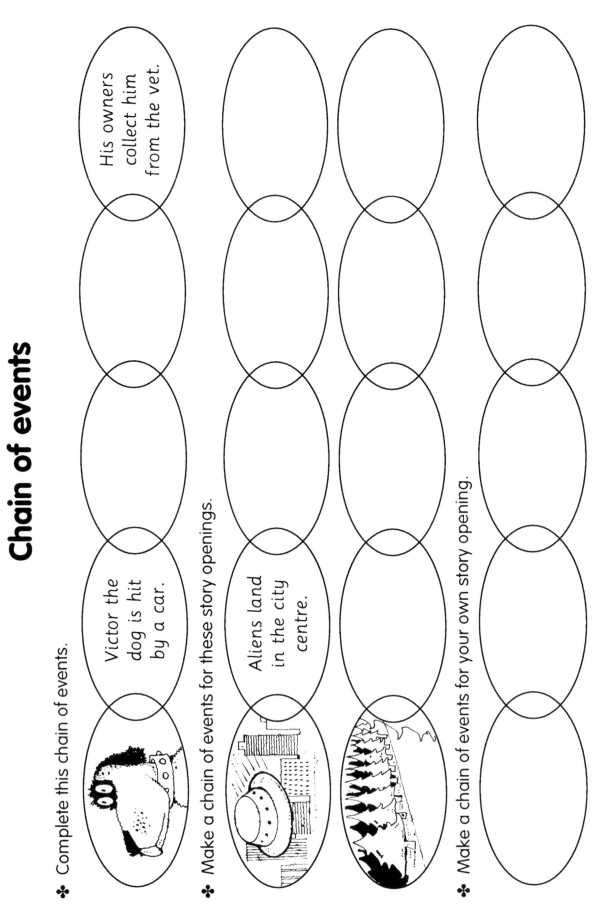

Victor the dog is hit by a car.

His owners collect him from the vet.

❖ Make a chain of events for these story openings.

Aliens land in the city centre.

❖ Make a chain of events for your own story opening.

Writing story endings

♣ Write a story ending for each of these pictures.
Try to use the way of ending which is written beside each picture.

Way to end
Sad ending

Way to end
Happy ending

Way to end
Happy ending

Way to end
**Happy ending
and a new
adventure starts**

Describing the seaside

✤ Look at this picture of the seaside. List as many words as you can in each box.

The sea
how it looks, feels, things in it

The sand
how it looks, feels, things on it

Colours around you

Sounds
you hear around you

Smells
from the sea and on the beach

✤ Describe the seaside in sentences. Try to use the words you have listed. Describe the sand, sea, smells, sounds and colours.

Describing the setting

✤ List words to describe your setting.

weather

objects

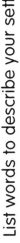

Drawing of my setting

colours

sounds

smells

Making fairy stories MODERN

❖ List four ingredients from a fairy story you know. Then try to think of four modern ingredients that could replace these. Use the bags of ideas if you need help.

Name of fairy story	
old ingredients	modern ingredients

❖ Write your own modern fairy story, using the modern ingredients on your chart.

SCHOLASTIC
www.scholastic.co.uk

Guess who puzzles

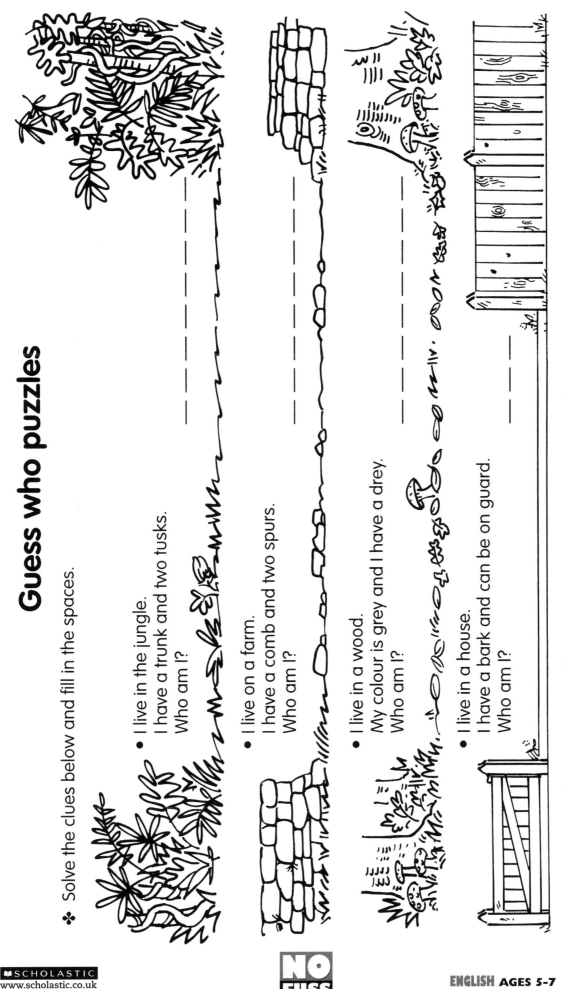

✤ Solve the clues below and fill in the spaces.

- I live in the jungle.
  I have a trunk and two tusks.
  Who am I?

- I live on a farm.
  I have a comb and two spurs.
  Who am I?

- I live in a wood.
  My colour is grey and I have a drey.
  Who am I?

- I live in a house.
  I have a bark and can be on guard.
  Who am I?

✤ Choose one of the answers above and paint or draw a picture of it.

Alliteration

Alliteration is when you use several words that start with the same **sound**.

♣ Finish the number poem below with lots of alliterations.

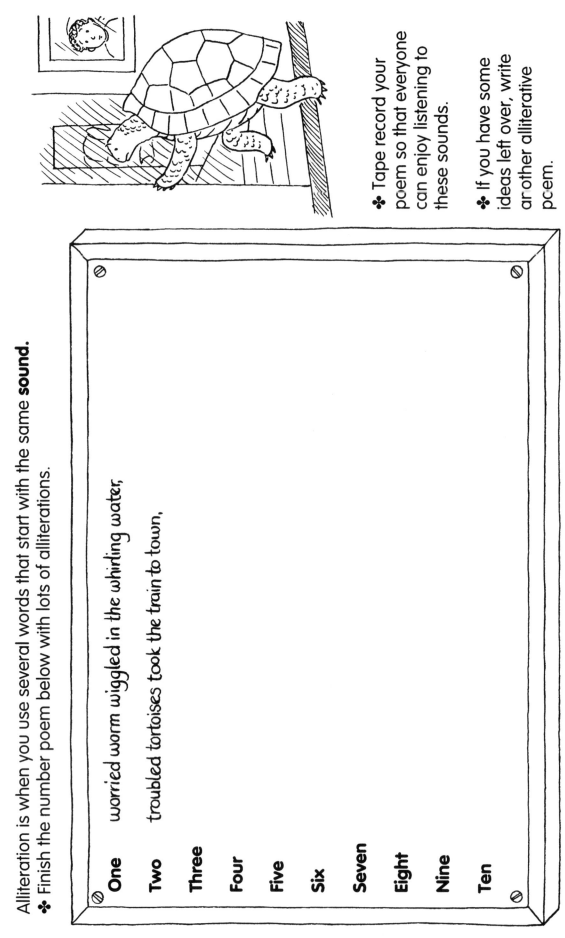

One   worried worm wiggled in the whirling water,

Two   troubled tortoises took the train to town,

Three

Four

Five

Six

Seven

Eight

Nine

Ten

♣ Tape record your poem so that everyone can enjoy listening to these sounds.

♣ If you have some ideas left over, write another alliterative poem.

SCHOLASTIC
www.scholastic.co.uk

Tongue-twister

a b c d e f g h i j k l m n o p q r s t u v w x y z

✤ Choose a letter and write a tongue-twister of your own on a strip of paper.

✤ Draw a picture of a face and stick your tongue-twister on to it.

Imran has made up a tongue-twister.

slick slippery snappy Sammy snake

He chose a letter 's'.
He found some words.
He tried them out.

slippery   shape

snappy   snoopy

slick   snake

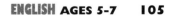

At the airport

● Look at the picture carefully.

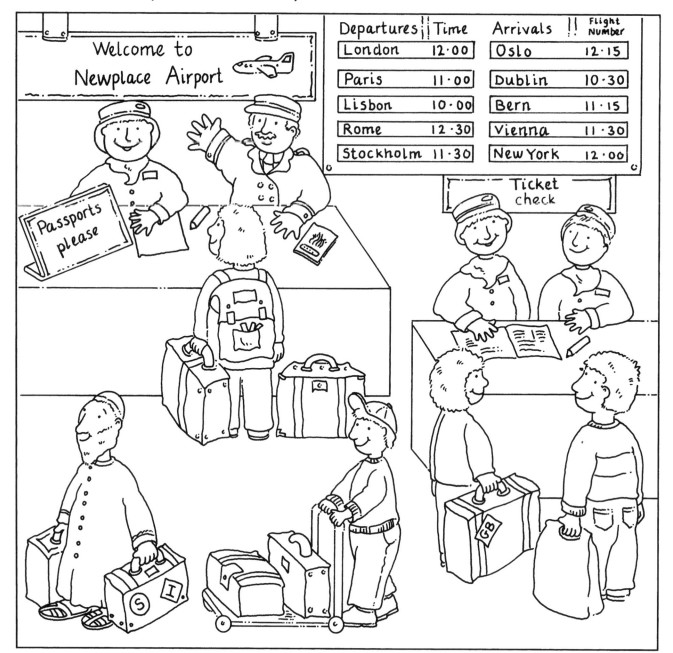

Departures	Time	Arrivals	Flight Number
London	12·00	Oslo	12·15
Paris	11·00	Dublin	10·30
Lisbon	10·00	Bern	11·15
Rome	12·30	Vienna	11·30
Stockholm	11·30	New York	12·00

Welcome to Newplace Airport

Passports please

Ticket check

● Answer these questions.

• What is the name of the airport?_____

• Where are the aeroplanes going?_____

_____

• Why do you need to check your ticket?_____

• What other desk do you need to go to? _____

Wet! Wet! Wet!

✤ Write a caption for each picture.

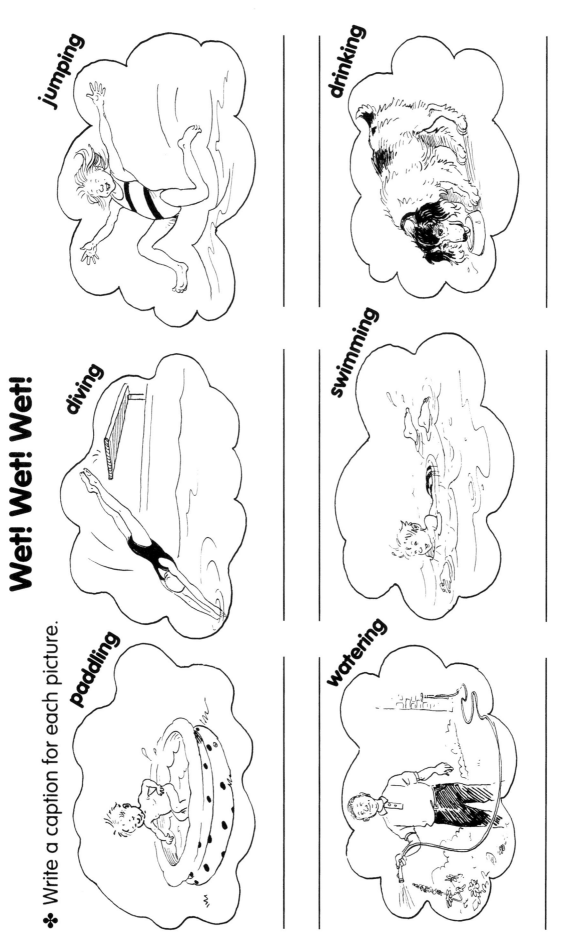

jumping

drinking

diving

swimming

paddling

watering

Do you know the parts of a flower?

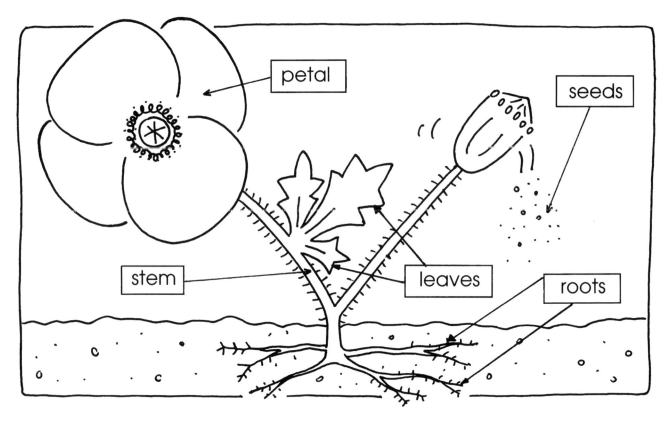

petal

seeds

stem

leaves

roots

● Write in the names of the parts of this flower.

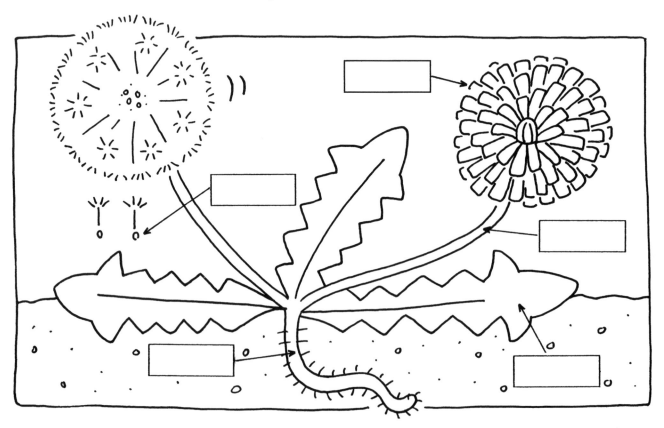

SCHOLASTIC
www.scholastic.co.uk

Name _____

A Roman soldier

A very long time ago Roman soldiers dressed like this.

● Label the picture. The writing below tells you all about him.

A Roman soldier wore a tunic and short leather trousers with a wide leather belt. On his feet he wore leather sandals. A Roman soldier always carried a dagger and a shield. His head was protected by a bronze helmet.

● What else can you find out about Roman soldiers?

The giant's list

The giant is going to cook his dinner.
● Help him to buy six things. He is very hungry.

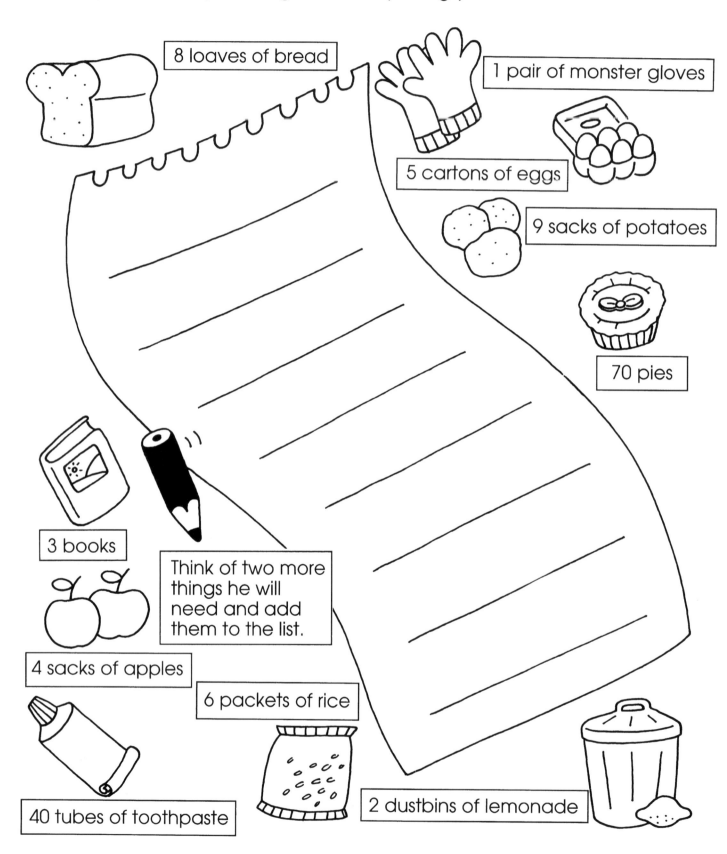

8 loaves of bread

1 pair of monster gloves

5 cartons of eggs

9 sacks of potatoes

70 pies

3 books

Think of two more things he will need and add them to the list.

4 sacks of apples

6 packets of rice

40 tubes of toothpaste

2 dustbins of lemonade

School rules

All schools have rules.

♣ Think of four rules that you have in your school. They might be classroom rules or playground rules.

♣ List them here.

♣ Choose a new rule that you think your school should have.

♣ Make a poster or notice telling everyone the new rule. Where would you put your notice?

Design a robot

● Choose some parts to make a robot. Instruct your partner how to draw your robot.

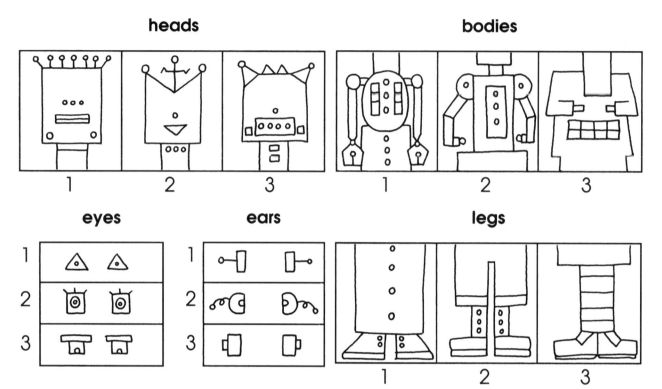

Spiral adventure

✤ Make up rules for this game.

✤ Make some notes and write your rules on the back of this sheet.

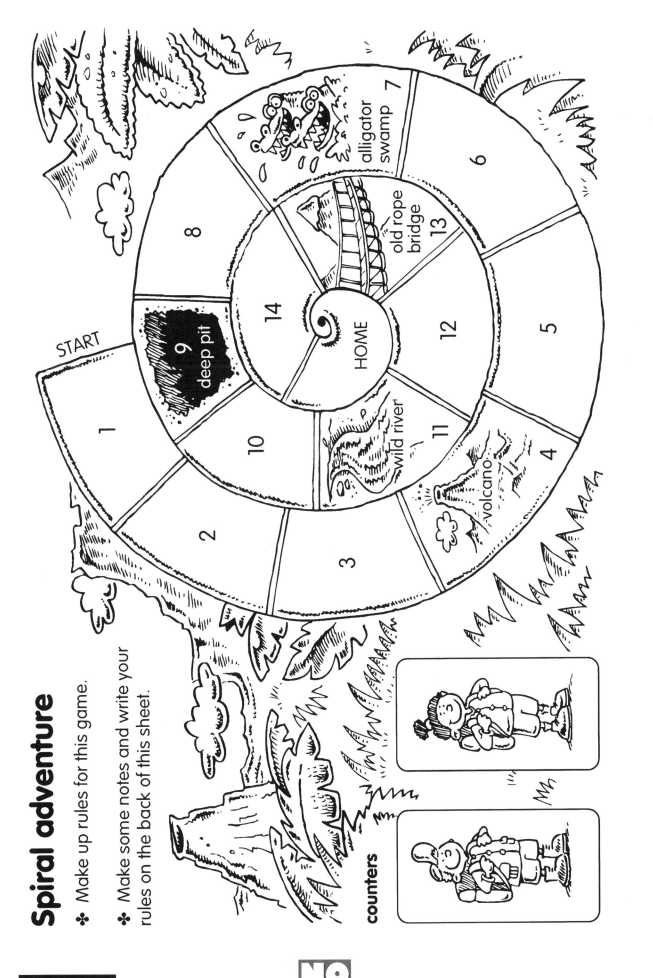

START

1

2

3

4

5

6

7 alligator swamp

8

9 deep pit

10

11 wild river

12

13 old rope bridge

14

HOME

volcano

counters

The alien planet

● Describe this picture. The words below will help you.

near	inside	in front of
beside	down	across	behind

The rocket has landed _____ a volcano. A spaceman

walks _____ the steps to get to the space buggy.

Some aliens are watching from _____ the rocks.

They live _____ the craters. The spaceman is going to

walk _____ the ground to put a flag _____

some large rocks _____ the aliens.

Name _____

Compass directions

● Hide a surprise for your partner somewhere in this classroom.
Give your partner directions to find it, using the compass.

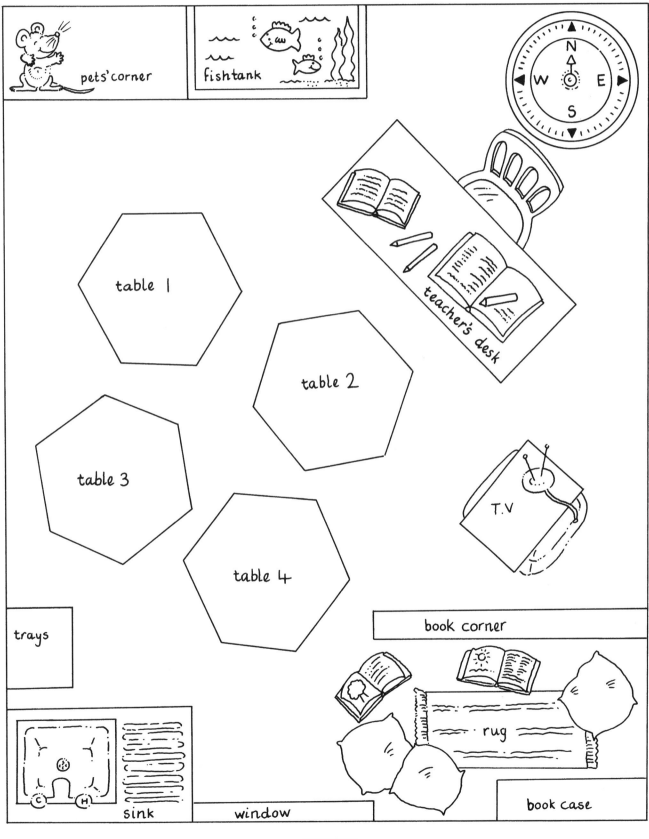

Fact and fiction

Both these books are about football. One is **fact** and one is **fiction**.

♣ Draw covers for two books about the same subject.
One book should be fact and one fiction.

♣ Write or draw a page from each book.

FACT

The first FA cup final to take place at Wembley was Bolton vs West Ham in 1923.

Fab Facts About Football

by J. Smith

FICTION

Wanda dribbled the ball towards the goal area. This was her big chance!

WANDA of the WANDERERS

by M. Ball

SCHOLASTIC
www.scholastic.co.uk

Name _____

Pen-friend from outer space

Your pen-friend from outer space has sent this picture to show you her home and family.

✤ Write to your pen-friend about where you live and your family.

My name is Toozoo. I live on planet Uoom. My planet has three suns. Here is a picture of my family and our pet. Do you like our house? Please tell me about your planet.

NO FUSS
PHOTOCOPIABLE

A postcard from a castle

● Finish the picture of the castle and colour it carefully.

● Finish writing this postcard and send it to someone you know.

Dear _____

   I am enjoying the school _____ to the castle. We went down into the _____.
They were dark and

_____

_____.

Love from _____

Address

_____

_____

_____

_____

NO FUSS
PHOTOCOPIABLE

Name _____

Greetings!

✤ Make a greetings card for a special occasion by cutting out, folding and colouring the part below. Inside write suitable greetings words. (You could use some of those shown on this page.)

Congratulations on your success!
... victory!
... great achievement!

Welcome back!
... home!
... to our school!
... to our club!

Many Happy Returns!
Merry Christmas!
Happy New Year!

Have a wonderful
... festival!
... birthday!
... celebration!
... holiday!

A very good morning!
... afternoon!
... evening!
Three cheers for friends!

NO FUSS
PHOTOCOPIABLE

An unusual folding abc

♣ Glance through your dictionary and choose an unusual word which starts with each letter of the alphabet.

♣ List them here.

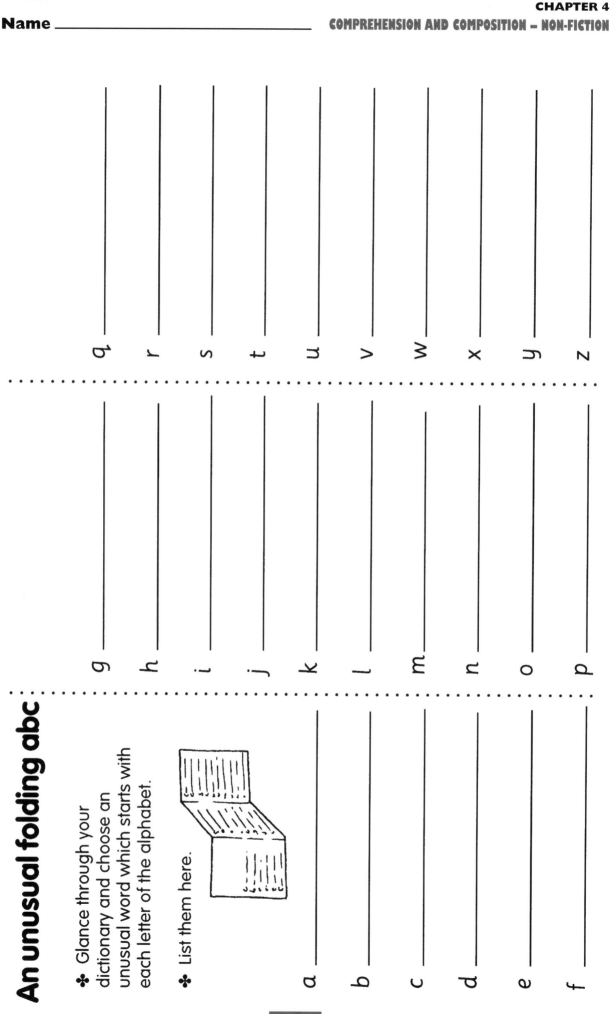

a

b

c

d

e

f

g

h

i

j

k

l

m

n

o

p

q

r

s

t

u

v

w

x

y

z

Reporting – the cycling accident

● Write a report about what has happened in the picture.

_____

_____

_____

_____

_____

_____

Writing charts from text

● Read the descriptions of the dog and the cat and fill in the chart at the bottom of the sheet.

The dog has short brown fur and a tail. He is small with pointed ears. He has a red collar and his name is Sam. He likes to sleep in his basket by the window. But he barks loudly when the postman comes down the path.

The cat has long grey fur and a long fluffy tail. She has bright blue eyes and pointed ears. She likes to sleep in a box under the table. She purrs happily when the sun shines. Her name is Sukey. She is a very friendly cat.

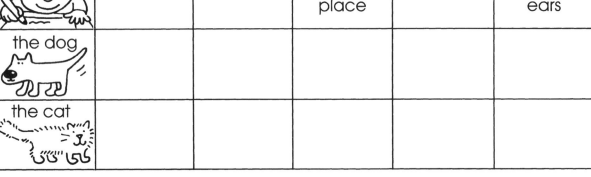

	name	colour	sleeping place	sounds	shape of ears
the dog					
the cat					

● Write about a cat or dog you know.

NO FUSS PHOTOCOPIABLE

SCHOLASTIC
www.scholastic.co.uk

Natural/man-made materials

● Look at the pictures. Think about which are made from natural materials and which from man-made materials. Fill in the grid.

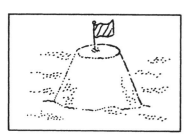

sand

tyre

stones

mug

Natural	Man-made

tree

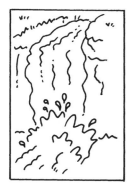

waterfall

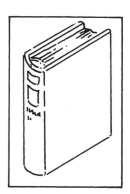

book

lunch box

coal

window

● Find some more things to add to your chart.

Finding out from charts

● Read this chart carefully. Write about the goldfish and the robin.

	size	colour	food	habitat	number of legs
a goldfish	small	orange red	flies insects fish food	pond or tank	none
a robin	small	brown and red	worms nuts bread	gardens nest	two

 A goldfish

 A robin

_____

_____

_____

_____

_____

_____

_____

● Look at books about them and see what else you can find out.

SCHOLASTIC
www.scholastic.co.uk

Frogs

♣ Find a book that will tell you about frogs. Look at the pictures below.
♣ Write a sentence about each picture, using the words to help you.

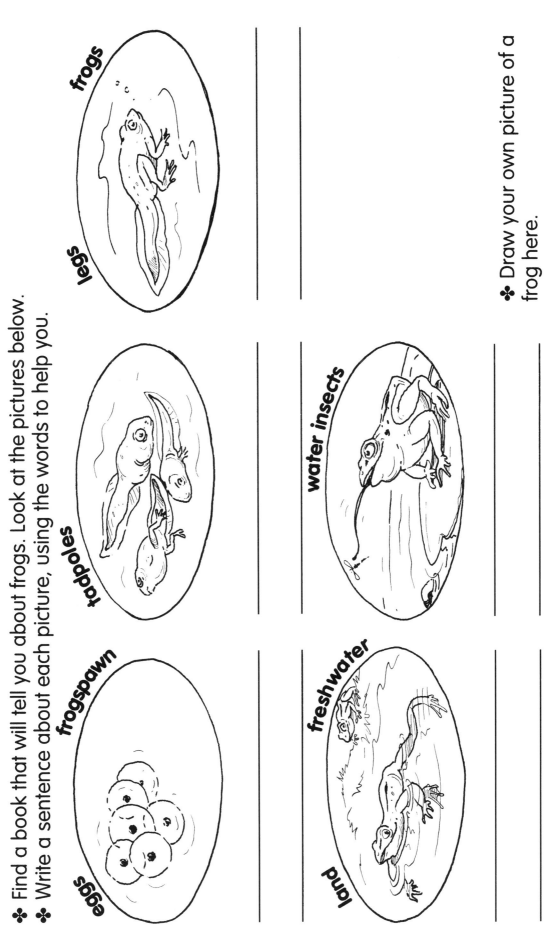

eggs — frogspawn

tadpoles

legs — frogs

land — freshwater

water insects

♣ Draw your own picture of a frog here.

Name _____

Read about the hedgehog

● Make some notes on the chart. Use the headings to help you.

Description	Habitat

Food	Other facts

Hedgehogs are small mammals. They have hard brown spines on their backs. If a hedgehog is frightened it rolls up into a ball. Their legs are short with five sharp claws on each foot.

Hedgehogs have long noses and a good sense of smell, but their eyesight is not very good. When they are hungry they eat slugs, spiders, snails, beetles and worms.

In the winter hedgehogs hibernate. They make nests from leaves. They find sheltered places, in ditches or under hedges, where they sleep in the cold weather.

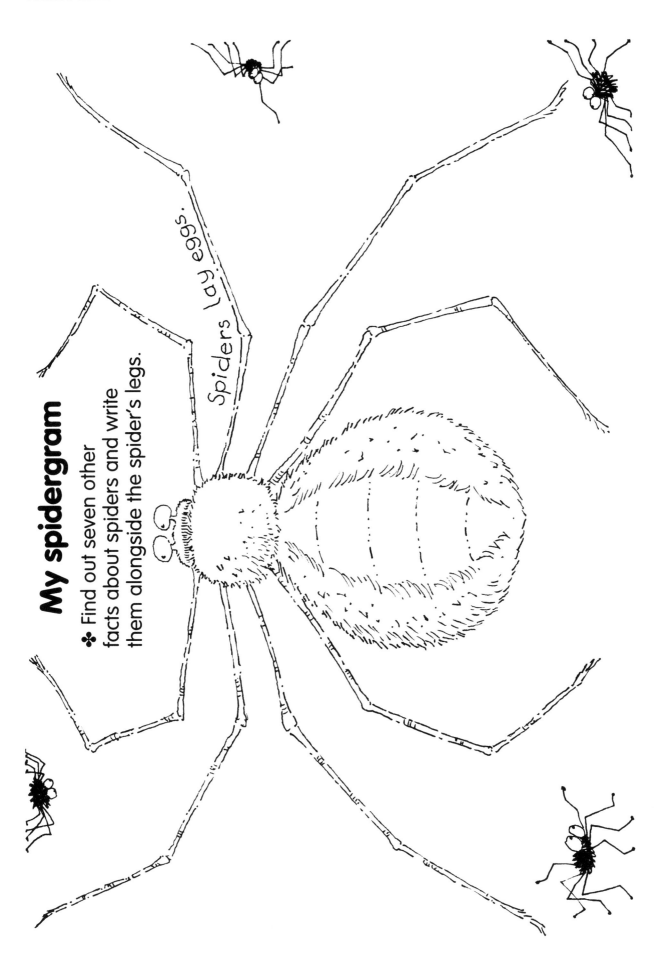

My spidergram

♣ Find out seven other facts about spiders and write them alongside the spider's legs.

Spiders lay eggs.

In this series:

ISBN 0-439-96548-9
ISBN 978-0439-96548-4

ISBN 0-439-96549-7
ISBN 978-0439-96549-1

ISBN 0-439-96550-0
ISBN 978-0439-96550-7

ISBN 0-439-96551-9
ISBN 978-0439-96551-4

ISBN 0-439-96552-7
ISBN 978-0439-96552-1

ISBN 0-439-96553-5
ISBN 978-0439-96553-8

To find out more, call: 0845 603 9091
or visit our website www.scholastic.co.uk